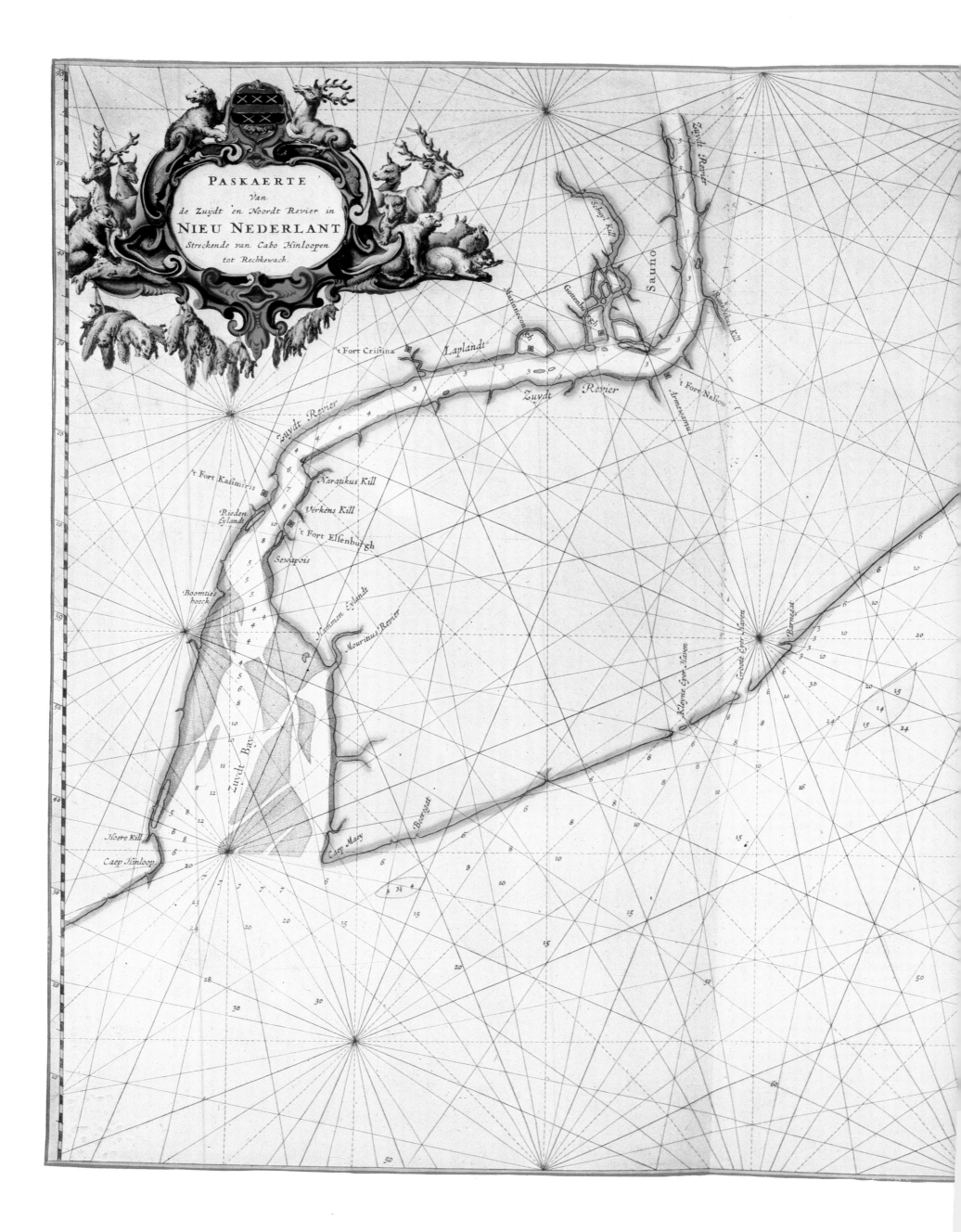

PASKAERTE
Van
de Zuydt 'en Noordt Revier in
NIEU NEDERLANT
Streckende van Cabo Hinloopen
tot Rechkewach.

Zuydt Revier

Schuyl Kill

Gottenburgh Eyl.

Sauno

Raukokus Kill

Matiniconck Eyl.

't Fort Cristina

Laplandt

Zuydt Revier

't Fort Nassou

Armewamus

't Fort Kasimiris

Naraticus Kill

Rieden Eylandt

Verkens Kill

't Fort Ellenburgh

Sewapois

Boomties hoeck

Nahmen Eylandt

Mouritius Revier

Zuydt Bay

Hoere Kill

Caep Hinloop

Caep Maey

Beeregat

Kleyne Eyer-Haven

Groote Eyer-Haven

Barnegat

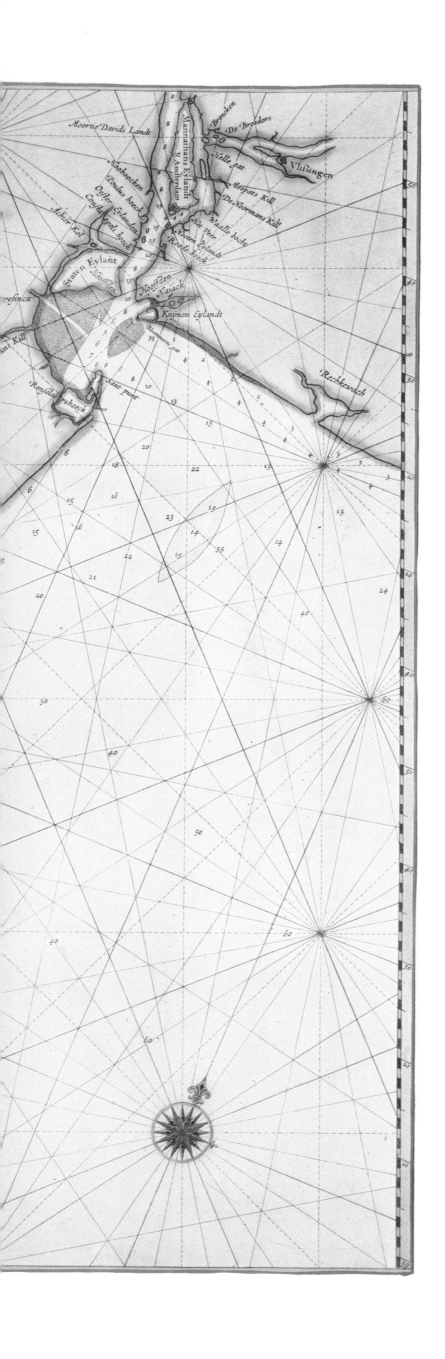

Early
Sea Charts

BY ROBERT PUTMAN

ABBEVILLE PRESS · PUBLISHERS · NEW YORK

Front cover:
William Barentsz's chart of the coasts of Sicily
and Malta, 1595 (Plate 4)

Frontispiece:
Pieter Goos's chart of the coast near
New York, 1666 (Plate 54)

Library of Congress Cataloging in Publication Data

Putman, Robert.
    Early sea charts.

    1. Nautical charts.   2. Maps, Early.   I. Title.
GA359.P83   1983   623.89'2'0222   83-8746
ISBN 0-89659-392-4

CONTENTS

INTRODUCTION

The fascination of the sea chart lies in its vital function aboard a ship. Its information about oceans and landforms has always meant the difference between safe and dangerous passage, between life and death. In an age of meticulously detailed maps and "push button" space travel, it is hard to imagine explorers leaving known waters with unreliable charts, crude navigational instruments, and only vague notions of what lies ahead. Yet for centuries mariners did just that. They composed their maps as they sailed, making unknown waters and territories familiar. However naive these documents may now seem, they reveal an intriguing part of the ongoing history of human exploration and discovery.

From surviving literature and artifacts we know that the classical civilizations of the Mediterranean, particularly that of Greece, were seafaring. Although only a few fragments of their *peripli* (seaman's guides) have survived, they suggest that nautical knowledge in antiquity was considerable. Like all such knowledge, it comprised a blend of written and spoken experience. Observations of seas, winds, and familiar coastlines passed from one generation of sailors to the next, thus maintaining and enlarging the gospel for safe dealings with the elements. Unfortunately, most of that information was lost to Europe during the Middle Ages, and had to be rediscovered.

That process of rediscovery began at the end of the Middle Ages, around 1200, when the first seaman's guide, sea chart, and compass appeared in the eastern region of the Mediterranean. The origins of these navigational aids are obscure. However, it is possible that they were passed to Italian merchants by the Arab civilizations that had held them since the fall of the Eastern Roman Empire.

The medieval seaman's guide, the *portolano* (literally "portbook") can be traced back to the *peripli* of antiquity. Its compass charts may have been copies of those used by Marinus of Tyre. If so, it would confirm that the Greeks understood the use of the magnetized needle.

The Italians were the first portolano chart makers; they were soon followed by the Catalans and the Majorcans of the Spanish Mediterranean coast. The discoveries of the Portuguese and the Spanish, which occurred at the end of the Middle Ages and heralded the modern age of sea exploration, encouraged the development of new navigational aids and improved charts. The Portuguese brought the sea-going nations of Europe their seaman's guides and portolano charts. These pilot books of west European waters were used from the fourteenth century on; they contained no charts, only sailing directions. They are called rutters from the French word *routier*, meaning chart or map. These rutters were all copied from others by hand, with amendments added by the new maker. At the end of the sixteenth century the first seaman's guide appeared; it combined sailing instructions and charts of coastal areas. These printed guides gave the mariner all the information he needed to navigate along Europe's coasts.

In the seventeenth century the plane chart came into common use aboard ship. It was based on the medieval portolano, with the addition of latitude and longitude lines. With this innovation two different systems of chart construction were combined. The discrepancies stemming from this combination were acceptable for charts with large-scale depictions of small areas, but not for the small-scale charts called *crossovers*. At the end of the sixteenth century advanced theoretical knowledge made it possible to construct charts suitable for navigating great distances, but it took a long time before these charts came into general use.

At the beginning of the second half of the seventeenth century the first printed sea atlases ap-

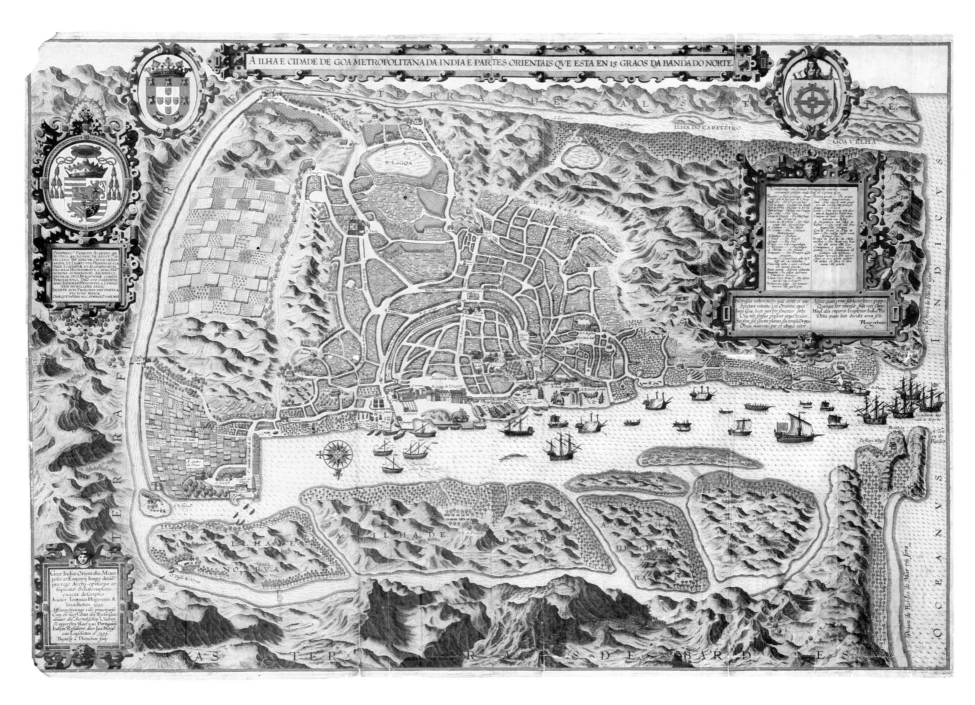

View of the capital of the
Portuguese colonies in
India, the town of Goa on
the island of Goa.
19 x 33″, copper engraving
on paper.
From the atlas *Itenerario*,
Voyage ofte Scheepvaert
by J.H. van Linschoten
(Amsterdam, 1596).

peared. The sea atlas is a collection of sea charts for general use; in most cases they were accompanied by a short description of the area depicted in the charts. Sea atlases in the seventeenth and eighteenth centuries were intended for the offices of merchants and for libraries. They were often colored by hand and luxuriously executed on thick paper with wide margins; the charts in the seaman's guides were printed on cheaper paper and usually were not colored. Seaman's guides, also called pilot books, are much scarcer today than sea atlases, despite the fact that they were printed in much larger quantities. Used and stored at sea under unfavorable conditions, they were usually thrown away when superseded by better and more modern charts. Charts on vellum, however, were better able to withstand the conditions at sea. When the information they contained became obsolete, these vellum charts were often used for another purpose, such as a bookbinding.

The development of chart making reflects changes in the prominence of maritime powers. The Italians became the first portolano chart makers during the height of prosperity in Florence, Venice, and Genoa. Similar achievements were attained by the Portuguese and Spaniards during their voyages of discovery and subsequent period of sea power. In the middle of the sixteenth century nautical cartography shifted to the mighty port of Dieppe, in France, and then, in the beginning of the seventeenth century, to Amsterdam. In the beginning of the next century, as Holland's international political role ended, England and France became the countries where the most advanced sea charts were made.

The development of ocean navigation depended on the formulation and use of increasingly accurate charts. So it is no surprise that the expansion of long-distance sea travel coincided with the introduction of charts based on the Mercator projection method. Despite their superiority over the plane chart and the globe, their general acceptance aboard ships did not occur for almost two centuries.

At the same time, two parallel developments occurred in nautical practice and scientific inquiry. The first improved coastal navigation, methods of dead reckoning at sea, and the use of portolano and plane charts. The second introduced more precise methods of astronomical navigation and chart making.

The following chapters explain the development of early sea charts by depicting the charts themselves. They follow a roughly chronological sequence. The first chapter encompasses the Mediterranean depicted by the classical cartographers and the first medieval chart makers. The second chapter concentrates on the southern part of the Atlantic Ocean in the fifteenth century, where the Portuguese made their first discoveries and developed the first astronomical instruments to be used at sea. The third chapter considers the West Indies, where the Spanish made their discoveries at the end of the fifteenth and the first half of the sixteenth centuries. On these voyages they encountered the problems of determining a ship's longitude and the variation of compass values.

The coastal waters of Western Europe saw the enormous maritime expansion of the countries bordering these waters during the sixteenth and seventeenth centuries. Chapter five concerns the east coast of North America. When it became clear in about 1520 that there was no sea passage to China in the Caribbean area, the search for this passage was continued in higher northern latitudes. All attempts were in vain, but the first settlements on the east coast of North America grew out of these endeavors. The discoveries of the coasts of the Indian Ocean and subsequent trading in the area, first by the Portuguese and afterward by the Dutch, are the subject of the sixth chapter. The last chapter is about the vast Pacific, its coasts and crossings.

SOUTHERN EUROPEAN WATERS

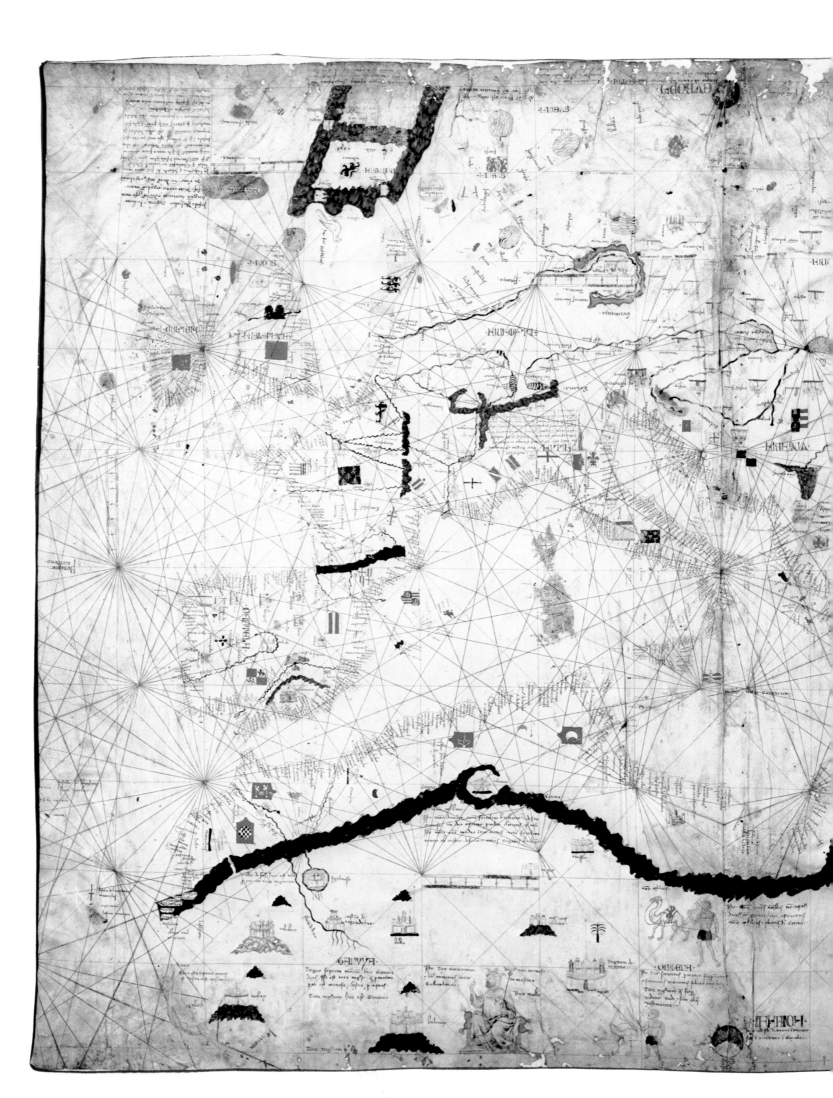

PLATE 1
Portolano of the
Mediterranean.
Angelino Dulcert (Majorca,
1339).
29¹¹⁄₁₆ x 40³⁄₁₆″, manuscript
on vellum.

Thales of Miletus (c. 600 B.C.) formulated the method of finding latitude by measuring the altitude of the sun or the Pole Star. He knew the earth to be a globe divided into five zones by the polar circles and the tropics. He understood the true nature of the solar eclipses and had calculated the distance between the two tropics.

Dicaearchus, a pupil of Aristotle, made the first attempt to graduate a map. On his map he drew a horizontal line from the Gades (the Strait of Gibraltar) in the west to the mountains bordering India in the east, with a perpendicular line through the island of Rhodes in a north-south direction.

Eratosthenes (c. 274–c. 194 B.C.), the librarian of Alexander the Great, described in his *Geography* the world as it was then known from the mouth of the Ganges in the east to Cape Guardafui on Africa's east coast in the south. His estimation of the circumference of the world was only four percent greater than it actually is.

About A.D. 140 Claudius Ptolemy summed up the existing geographical knowledge of his time in his famous work, the *Geographia*. He made two mistakes that would have important consequences thirteen centuries later. He overestimated the extent of the known world, thus underestimating that of the unknown world; in his conception there was no place for the American continents. His second mistake was drawing a vast, theoretical Southland counterbalancing the land masses of the Northern Hemisphere. This Southland connected Africa with China, thus making the Indian Ocean an inland sea.

Ptolemy based his effort partly on the work of Marinus of Tyre, who made sea charts and wrote sailing directions. After the fall of the Roman Empire, all this knowledge was inherited by the Arabs, with whom it remained, inaccessible to European culture for many centuries.

The first portolano appeared in Italy at the end of the thirteenth century. There is evidence that the charts of Marinus of Tyre still existed in the middle of the tenth century, and it might be that the Venetians or the Genoese, who traded with the Arabs in the eastern Mediterranean, had seen these sea charts and bought or copied them. This indeed could be the link between classical and modern nautical science.

The portolano chart depicted here is one of the few surviving fourteenth-century sea charts. The maker, Angelino Dolceti, probably a native of Genoa who was known to have worked on Majorca, was called Dulcert by the Spanish. The chart is dated 1339. It shows a large area: the Mediterranean, the Black Sea, and North Africa with the Canary and the Azores islands—long

before their "official" discovery in 1427. In the lower right-hand corner, in red, the Red Sea is depicted. Ireland, England, and the West European continent including Scandinavia and the Baltic are also shown.

There is a striking difference between the accurate delineation of the Mediterranean, the Black Sea, and the southern part of the Atlantic coastline and the description of their ports and the meager description of the interior of the European continent and the North Atlantic coastal areas. Ireland, the southern part of England, and the Atlantic coasts up to Flanders are more or less correctly depicted; farther north the representation is rather confusing. The semicircle in red represents the mountains of Bohemia, and from there the river Rhine flows west! The brown rectangle is Norway, the two red lions represent Sweden, and the legend west of Norway is related to Iceland.

Three sovereigns, seated on their thrones, are depicted: in North Africa Rey Melli, in the east the queen of Sheba, and in the upper right the emperor Usbeck. In Palestine the Holy Sepulcher is shown.

Mariners found their way at night by means of the only fixed point in the sky, the North Star. By keeping a constant bearing on this star, they were sure to steer a steady course. The compass needle, magnetized by a lodestone, made it possible to do the same in daylight. The seaman did not necessarily understand the phenomenon, but he understood its application to finding direction at sea.

The first compasses were mere bowls of water which held a floating magnetized needle—hardly an instrument fit for use aboard a ship. But from the fourteenth century on, ships carried a sea compass that had a compass rose attached to a magnetized needle. This rotated on a vertical axis in a wooden box. The eight cardinal points were drawn on the compass rose. From ancient times in the Mediterranean the directions were named after the winds that blew the ships on a steady course in that direction. The Italians, for instance, named the north wind the *Tramontana*, referring to the Alps, and the other winds according to their particular origins. The compass

was mounted in gimbals to keep it level during the movements of the ship.

The roses on the chart became compass roses, as the rhumb lines represented courses of the compass. The rhumb lines on the chart permitted a pilot to set a course from his port of departure to his destination, and the compass enabled him to keep it. The precision of such a compass chart depended, first, on the exactness with which the directions were determined and, second, on the exactness with which the distance covered was measured. Considering the inaccurate tools of the time, one can only marvel at the skill of these early nautical cartographers.

The Italians, particularly the Venetians, the Genoese, and the Florentines, were the first portolano chart makers. After 1350 they were joined by the Majorcans who formed, together with the cartographers of Barcelona, the chart makers of the School of Catalan. Coastal navigation is the oldest form of navigation. Rooted in classical antiquity, it was practiced long before mariners dared to leave their trusted home waters. It was based on the observation of known features of the coastal area, like navigation routes, prevailing winds, currents, coastal profiles, anchor grounds, shoals, rocks, etc. For centuries this information was passed verbally from the experienced pilot to his apprentice. In the thirteenth century, written pilot guides appeared in the Mediterranean. They were called *portolanos*, and they gave the seaman all the information he needed for navigation. The oldest-known portolano is dated 1296 and is a copy of another pilot guide from about 1250.

The pilot guides of antiquity, the *peripli*, must have been models for these medieval pilot books. The portolano did not contain charts in the form in which we know them, but coastal profiles were drawn in the text.

Simultaneous with the first portolano appeared the first hand-drawn chart, which functioned as the image of an area. These manuscript charts are rather confusingly called portolano charts or compass charts, and they are based on the concepts of direction and distance. Knowing the course held and the distance covered on a voyage from one port to another, it is then possible to position in a chart the second port in relation

12

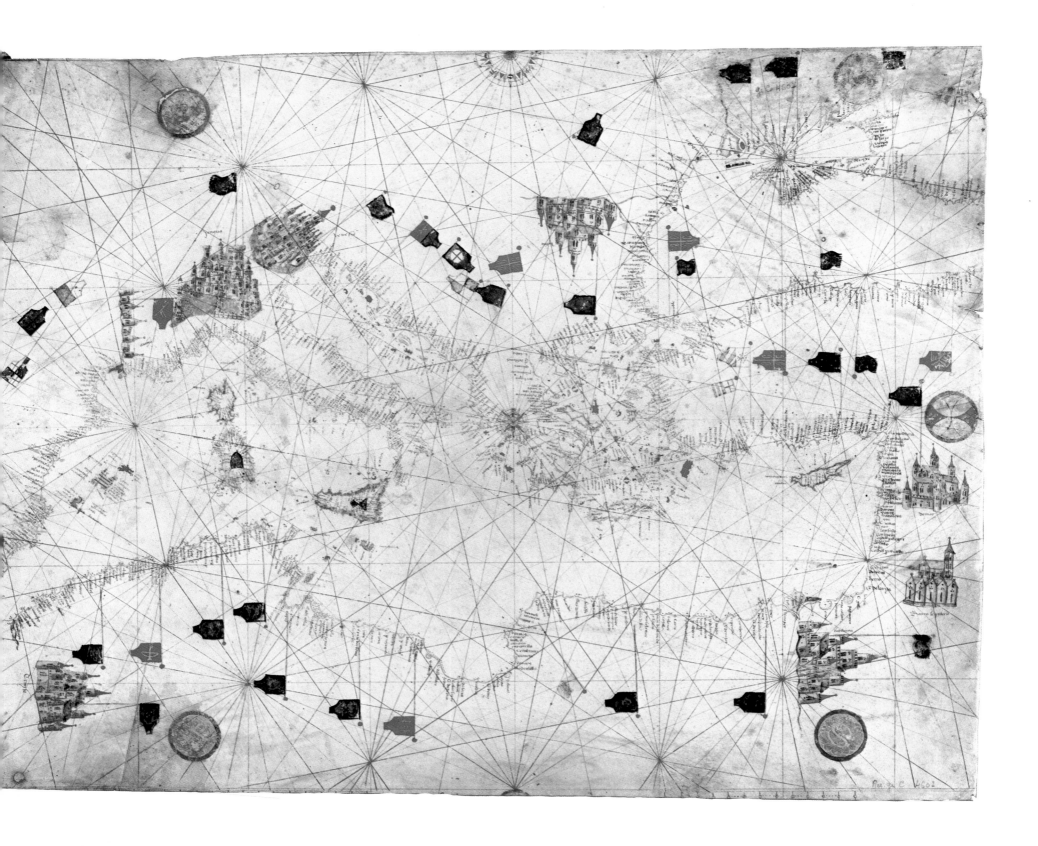

to the point of departure. The medieval cartographer started by drawing a number of wind roses on a specially prepared skin of a sheep or a goat; they gave the directions of the main winds of the Mediterranean. From these roses so-called rhumb lines were drawn, indicating courses held when sailing with these winds. Starting from one point—the port where he worked—the cartographer drew the coastlines in the position he knew them to have in relation to his starting point.

It is said that these charts appeared after, and because of, the introduction of the compass by the Arabs in the twelfth century. But the roses on the first portolano charts were not compass roses but rather wind roses. The theory that the first medieval charts were copies of charts made in antiquity and kept by the Arabs may be more plausible.

In the early animal skin map (plate 2) on which this early portolano chart of the Mediterranean is drawn, the maker of this chart has written *Gabriel de Vallsecha la affeta en Mallorcha ai MCCCCXXXXVII* ("Made by Gabriel de Vallsecha at Majorca in 1447"). Along the coasts the names of ports are given, and the most important ports are indicated with a standard. The most important cities of the fifteenth century—Grenada, Avignon, Genoa, Venice, Vienna, Damascus, Jerusalem, Cairo (named Babilonia), and Tlemcen—are drawn. The most important rivers—the Rhone, the Danube, and the Nile—are indicated. The Atlantic coasts of Europe are omitted. One main wind rose situated in Greece and sixteen secondary roses with rhumb lines radiating from them enabled the seaman to find the course to be steered.

The six "disks of the winds," indicating the main winds in the Mediterranean, are a particular feature of Catalan charts.

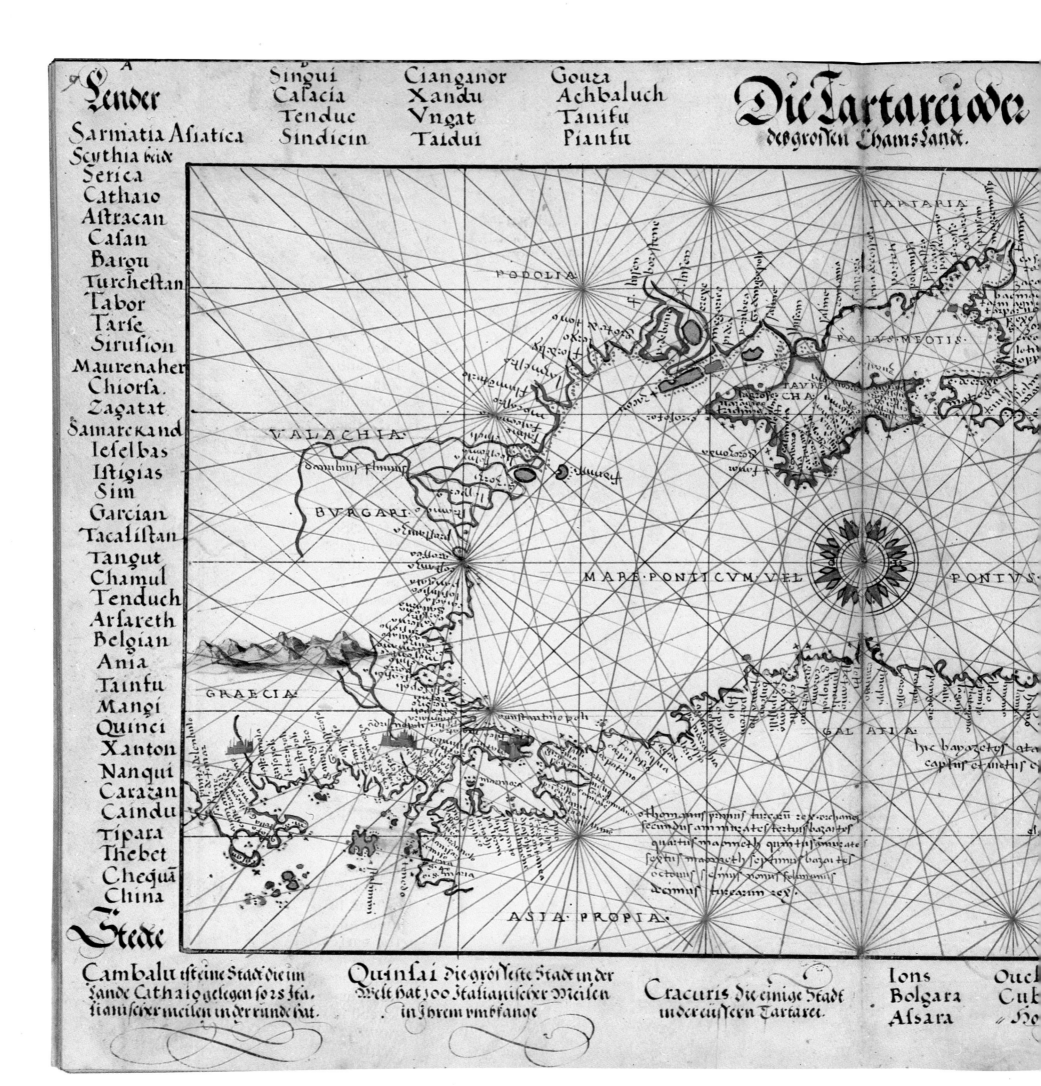

PLATE 3
Portolano of the Black Sea.
Battista Agnese (Venice,
1554).
29¹¹⁄₁₆ x 45¹¹⁄₁₆″, manuscript
on vellum.

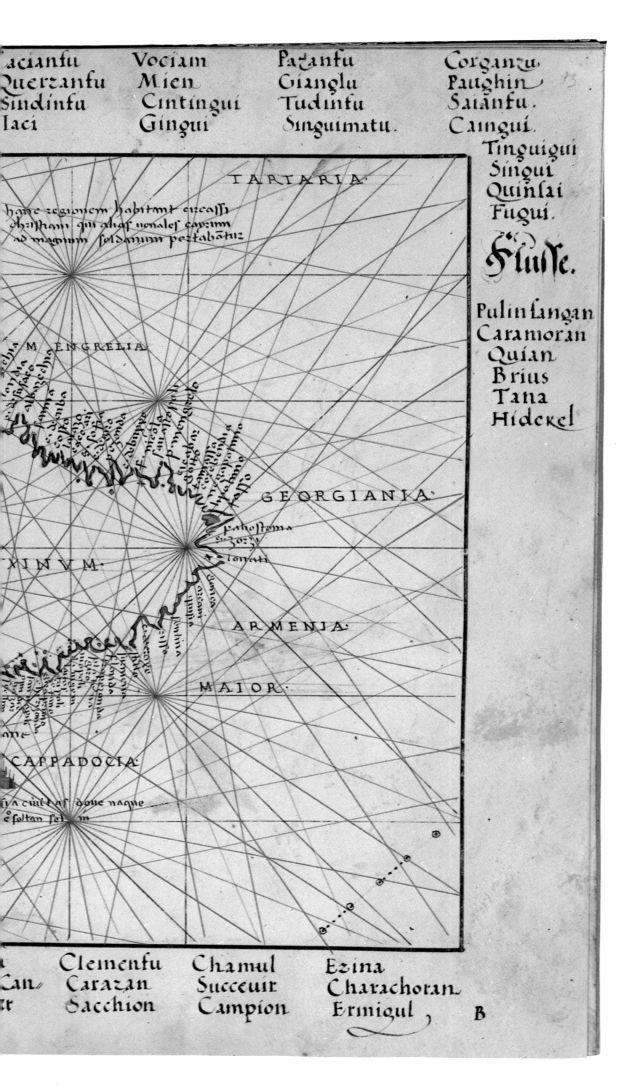

At the end of the thirteenth century, Islam blocked the traditional trade routes to the Far East through the Red Sea. At the same time, the Mongol conquest of a vast empire from the Black Sea in the west to the China Sea in the east opened up a commercial route overland to the countries of the Far East. The starting point for the route through central Asia was the port of Tańa on the border of the Sea of Azov in the north, the land route through Mongol Persia to the Indian Ocean began in Trebizond on the southern coast of the Black Sea. The Italians, and in particular the Venetians and Genoese, dominated these profitable trade routes. After 1453, the year the Turks took Constantinople, the Italians were gradually excluded from the Black Sea. At the same time the Portuguese opened the sea route south of the African continent to the Far East and displaced the Italians in the trade with the countries of the Indian Ocean and the China Sea.

Battista Agnese, who worked between 1536 and 1564, belongs to the Italian school of portolano chart makers. He was a prolific cartographer, and more than seventy atlases, some with more than ten charts, are extant.

A native of Genoa, he worked in Venice, at that time the center of commercial chart making. His abilities as draughtsman as well as illuminator were considerable. The early portolano sea charts, like Agnese's, depicted almost correctly the coastlines of the Black Sea.

For unknown reasons seventeenth-century charts deviated from this correct delineation of the Black Sea. It was the Dutchman Cornelius Cruys, admiral of the Russian fleet, who around 1700 corrected these mistakes.

This finely executed chart of the Black Sea gives an impression of the quality of the work of the early Italian portolano chart makers. It is part of an atlas with twelve sea charts and thirteen land maps. The chart is covered with rhumb lines, enabling the mariner to set a course. The legend in the Black Sea reads MARE PONTICUM VEL PONTIUS EUXINUM. In the borders a later hand has written in German the names of countries, cities, and rivers.

Dutch navigation in the Mediterranean was negligible until the last decade of the sixteenth century. When they did start to sail the Mediterranean, they needed pilot guides with Dutch texts. Italian portolano atlases that contained, in general, eight or nine manuscript charts were available. One of these atlases must have been the model for Willem Barentsz's *Caertboeck van de Midlandtsche Zee* (Chartbook of the Mediterranean), made in 1595. It was the first printed book with charts of the Mediterranean. Besides the drawings in the text, it contained one chart of the whole Mediterranean and eight charts of parts of it. The chart of the whole area was by Petrus Plancius and was engraved by Hendrik Hondius. The other nine charts were compiled by Barentsz himself, probably using material by Plancius. The engravings are by the well-known engraver Pieter van de Keere.

Little is known of Willem Barentsz except for the last years of his life. In 1594 a contemporary recorded that Barentsz, at that time a citizen of Amsterdam, had been born on the island of Terschelling. He must have been a pilot experienced with the Mediterranean as well as northern seas, and he probably belonged to the group of mariners instructed by Petrus Plancius in mathematical navigation.

He was selected by Plancius to serve as a pilot aboard a ship fitted out by the Amsterdam merchants to search for a northeast passage to China. Three voyages were made, all in vain. The last voyage was forced to winter on Novaja Zeml'a, and Barentsz died from exhaustion on the way back in an open boat. These dramatic events are related in the narrative of Gerrit de Veer, a subordinate of Barentsz. Barentsz's fame is due to his chart of the Arctic regions in polar-stereographic projection, which shows the discoveries of the Dutch in that region.

The folio-size *Caertboeck* supplemented Lucas Waghenaer's *Spieghel der Zeevaerdt*. Together they covered all European waters.

Chart number nine of the pilot guide depicts the seas around Sicily with insets of the principal ports. It shows the skill of one of the most accomplished engravers of his time, Petrus Kaerius or Pieter van de Keere.

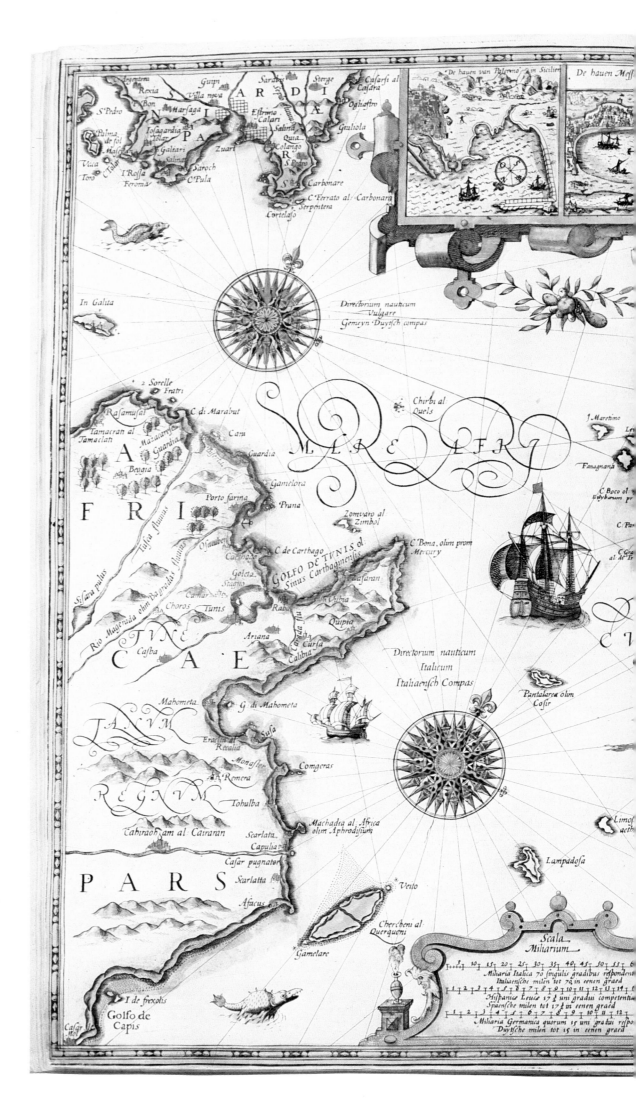

PLATE 4
Sea chart of the coasts of
Sicily and Malta, the islands
in the vicinity, and parts of
Calabria, Sardinia, and
Africa, with the important
ports of the area in the
insets.
William Barentsz
(Amsterdam, 1595).
16⅛ x 21¹¹/₁₆″, copper
engraving on paper.
From the pilot guide *Caert-boeck van de Midlandtsche Zee.*

PLATE 5
Sea chart of the island of
Malta.
Johannes Janssonius
(Amsterdam, 1650).
17⅝ x 21¼″, copper
engraving on paper.
From the atlas *Atlantis
Majoris, Quinta Pars, Orbis
Maritimus.*

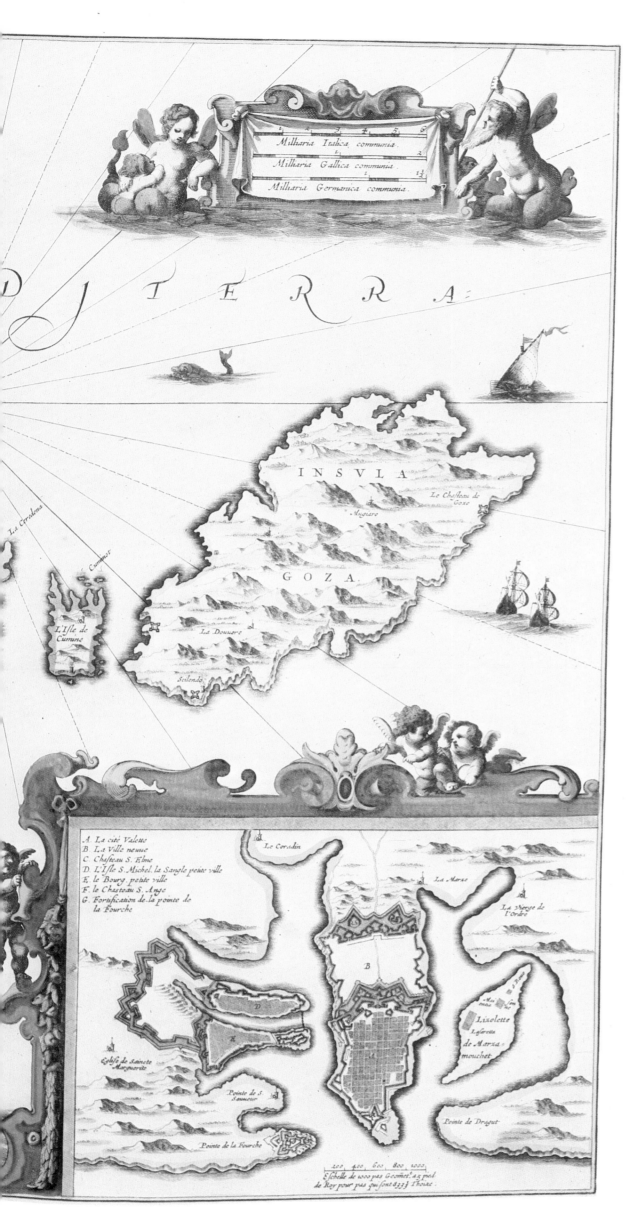

EQUINOCTIAAL KOMPAS

Johannes Janssonius (1588–1664) was the lifetime rival of the Blaeus. But unlike Willem Blaeu, who started his career as a seller of sea charts, Johannes Janssonius's main interest never lay in the field of hydrographic publications.

After the death of Jodocus Hondius in 1612, his son, Hendrik Hondius, together with his brother-in-law Janssonius, continued to publish the *Mercator-Hondius Atlas*, containing maps of the known world. When the plates of this atlas came into the Blaeus' hands, they had new copies cut. It developed into the *Atlas Novus*, first published in 1638. The outstanding feat of Janssonius in the hydrographic field is that he enlarged this *Atlas Novus* in 1650 with a fifth volume, a sea atlas named the *Water-Weereldt*. This was the first sea atlas—a collection of charts in folio size to serve as a general-purpose atlas—published in the Dutch republic; all previous publications had been pilot guides. He was followed by other publishers of pilot books, for example, Hendrik H. Doncker in 1659 and Pieter Goos in 1666.

Unlike the pilot guide, the sea atlas was not meant at first to be used aboard a ship; it was intended for use in the libraries and offices of merchants. The chart of Malta depicted here comes from the sea atlas published by Johannes Janssonius and, with its decorative character, is more than simply a navigational aid.

In its long history Malta saw many foreign masters come and go. With its strategically important location halfway between Italy and Africa's north coast, it played an important role in Mediterranean shipping. That is why Janssonius had a separate chart of Malta in his atlas. Janssonius included in his introduction a beautiful wind rose with a description of the nature and the names of the most important winds.

The compass rose is derived from the wind rose. It appeared for the first time in manuscript portolano charts of the Mediterranean. In these early wind roses only four or eight directions were drawn; the rose with thirty-two points is of a later date. These main points were given the names of the respective Mediterranean winds blowing from these directions.

The north wind is called *Tramontana*, ("across the mountains") by the Italians. The *Greco* comes from the northeast, and the eastern wind is called the *Levante*. The southeastern wind is named the *Sirocco*, and the wind from the south, the *Ostro* (in Greek it is called *Notus*, which means "humid" since this wind is generally warm and humid).

The southwest wind is called *Africus* or *Libecia*—"the one that comes from Lybia." The wind from the west is the *Ponente* (the Greek call it *Zephyrus*, for this wind brings life in spring; likewise the French call this wind *Le Vente Feuilleret*, "wind of the leaves"). The northwestern wind is called the *Maestro* (in French, the *Mistral*).

PLATE 6
Wind-rose.
Johannes Janssonius
(Amsterdam, 1650).
17⅛ x 21¼", copper
engraving on paper.
From the atlas *Atlantis
Majoris, Quinta Pars, Orbis
Maritimus.*

20

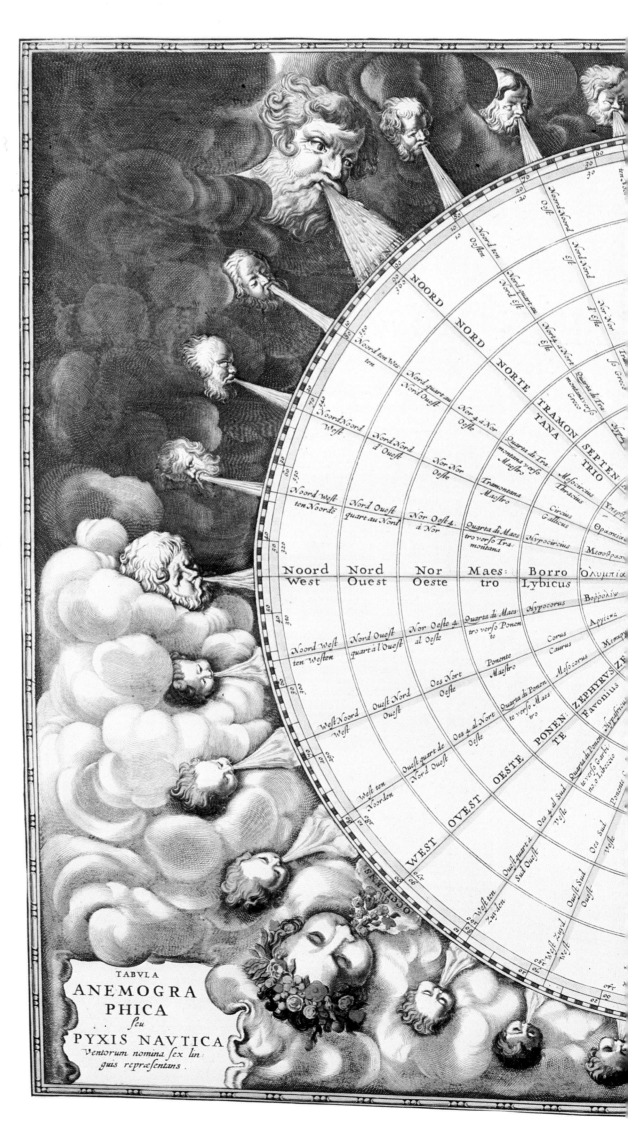

AMSTELODAMI
Apud Ioan. Ianſſonium.

ZEE-KOMPAS

21

At the end of the seventeenth century, Willem III, stadholder of the United Provinces of the Northern Netherlands, known to the English as King William III, commissioned his favored artist Romeijn de Hooghe to embellish nine manuscript charts of English origin depicting the seas south of Holland. This area was the stage for the battles between Willem's fleets and those of his French foe Louis XIV.

Romeijn de Hooghe was an accomplished Dutch artist, known for his finely executed etchings of the important events in the life of his king. He decorated the nine charts, which together compose the *Atlas Maritime*, with beautiful cartouches and insets showing harbors and cities. Another engraver, who remains unknown, cut the plates after the manuscript charts were drawn. The atlas was published by the well-known Amsterdam publisher Pieter Mortier in 1694. The last chart of the *Atlas Maritime* is of the Mediterranean; it also shows the Atlantic coasts of Spain, Portugal, and Morocco with the

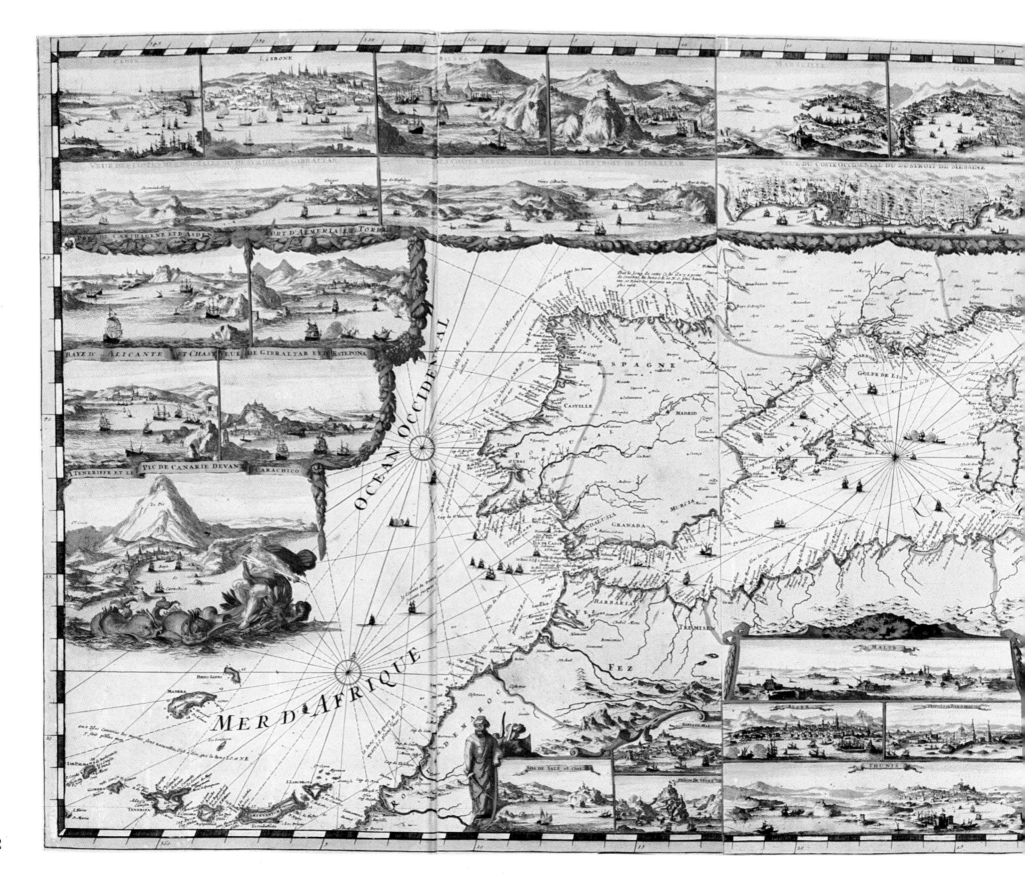

Canary Islands and, in the far right, the Black Sea. With its thirty-eight insets of the most important ports of the Mediterranean, the chart is the most decorative sea chart printed in seventeenth-century Amsterdam and a tribute to the memory of that exceptionally skilled artist, Romeijn de Hooghe.

PLATE 7
Chart of the Mediterranean, with 38 views of ports.
Pieter Mortier and Romeijn de Hooghe (Amsterdam, 1694).
23 x 54¾″, copper engraving on paper.
From the sea atlas *Atlas Maritime*.

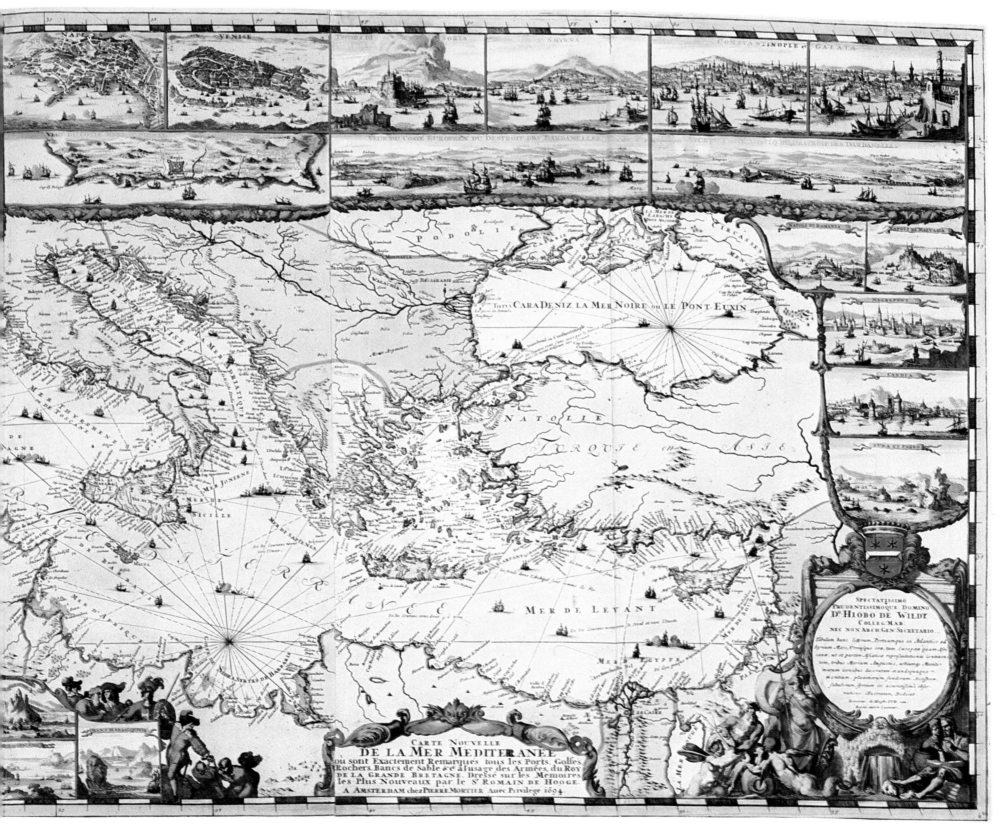

When Johannes van Keulen, the founder of the Dutch publishing house by that name, retired in 1704, he was succeeded by his son Gerard van Keulen.

Unlike his father, Gerard van Keulen was a gifted mathematician and showed his abilities in his excellent charts based on the Mercator projection. He became hydrographer to the Dutch East Indies Company in 1714. The van Keulens remained chart makers to the East Indies Company until the company was liquidated at the end of the eighteenth century.

Gerard van Keulen was also a prolific cartographer. Not only was he responsible for many of the 600 printed charts issued by the van Keulen publishing house, but between 1706 and 1726—the years during which he managed the firm—he also compiled at least 500 manuscript charts. This vast collection of charts, all in a uniform size of 60 x 100 cm., covered all the coastal areas of the world; many of them are large-scale and show in precise detail the location of harbors and coastal routes at the beginning of the eighteenth century.

Gerard died in 1726, leaving the firm to his son Johannes II, who contributed to the firm's fame by publishing the sixth and last part of the pilot guide, the *Zeefakkel*, in 1753.

PLATE 8
The city and harbor of
Barcelona.
Gerard van Keulen
(Amsterdam, 1724).
23⅝ x 47¼″, manuscript on
paper.

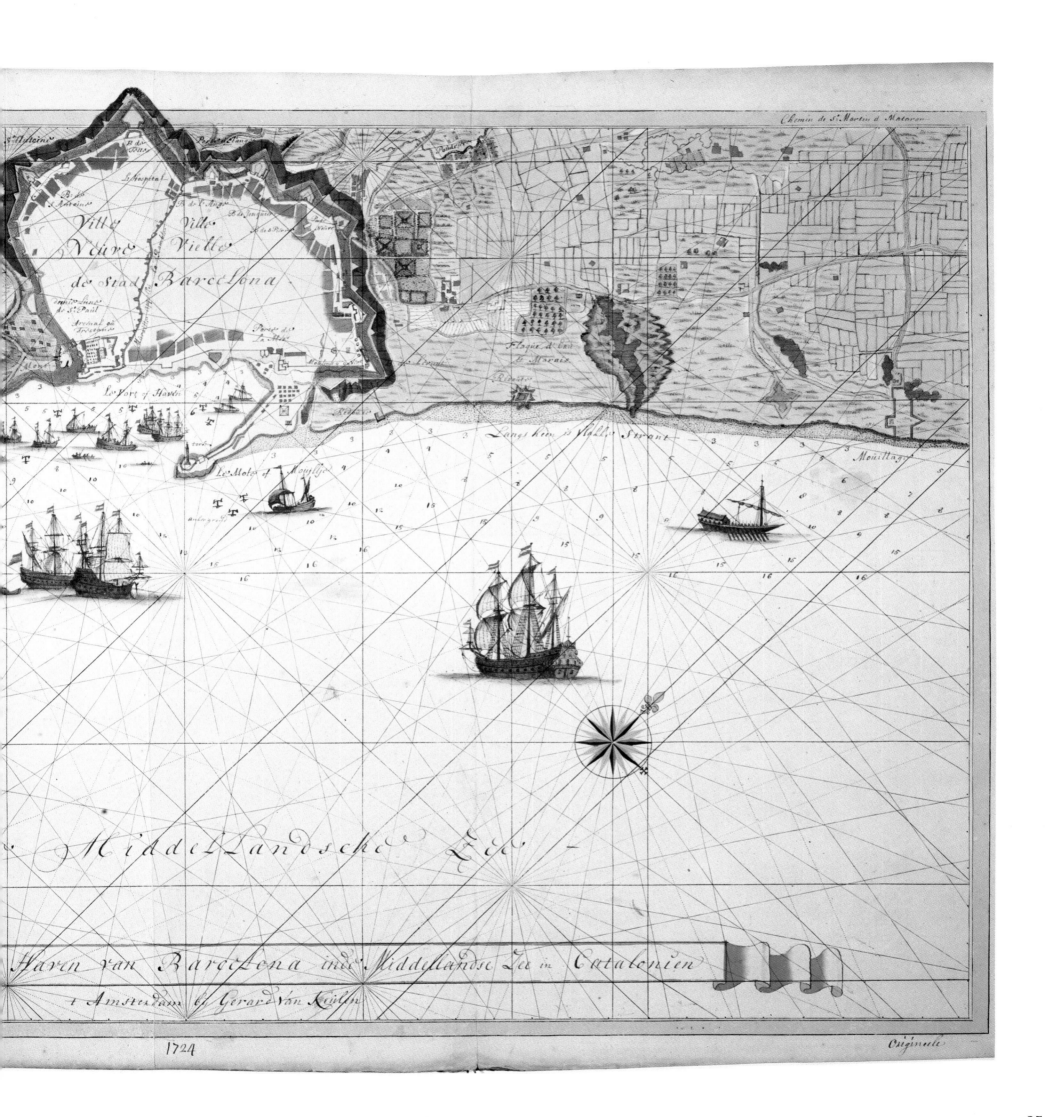

Haven van Barcelona inde Middellandse Zee in Catalonien

t Amsterdam by Gerard van Keulen

1724

Originele

25

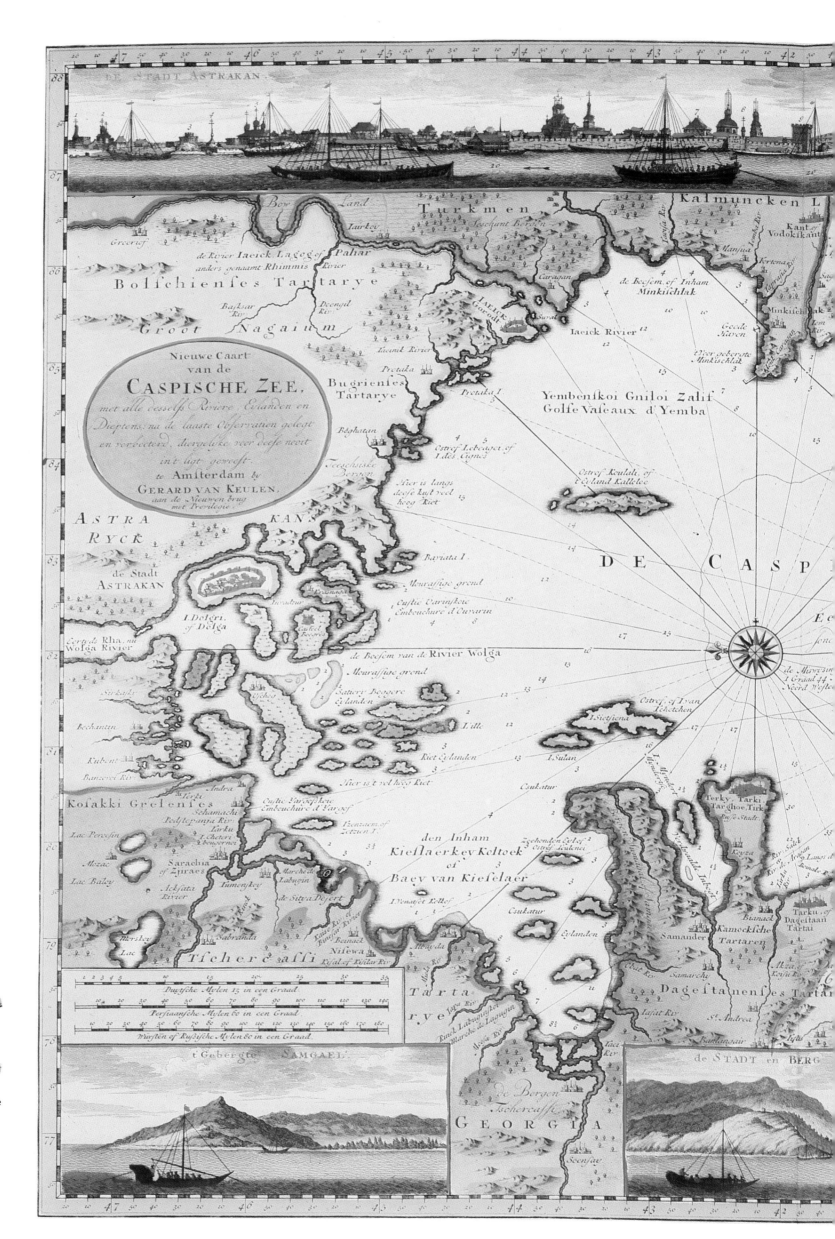

PLATE 9
Chart of the coasts of the
Caspian Sea.
Gerard van Keulen
(Amsterdam, 1734).
21⅝ x 22⁷⁄₁₆″, copper
engraving on paper.
From the pilot guide *De
Nieuwe Groote Ligtende
Zeefakkel.*

The Greek Hecataeus of Miletus thought the Caspian Sea to be part of the ocean surrounding the earth. The great Greek historian of the fifth century B.C., Herodotus of Halicarnassus, knew the Caspian to be an inland sea, but 500 years later the Roman historian Pliny thought that the Caspian was connected with the polar sea north of the Asian continent.

From 1206 on, the Mongolians commanded by Genghis Khan conquered the vast plains of inner Asia. After devastating Hungary in 1242, they withdrew from Europe. In the middle of the century European ambassadors visited the court of the Khans, north of the Gobi desert. The most famous of these travelers was Marco Polo, who at the end of the thirteenth century stayed for many years at the court of Kublai Khan and whose writings were for many centuries the most important source of information on the countries and people of the Asian continent.

In the Catalan world map of 1375 the Caspian Sea is depicted. It was the English who in the fifteenth century traveled from the White Sea via Moscow to the south and then sailed the Caspian Sea. A narrative by the Englishman Anthony Jenkins has been preserved. Marco Polo wrote about the Caspian Sea, or the Sea of Baku, as an inland sea with a circumference of 2,800 miles. He described the abundant sturgeon and salmon and the fountains of oil at Baku. He wrote, "The use made of it is not for the purpose of food, but as an unguent for the cure of cutaneous distempers in men and cattle, as well as other complaints; and it is also good for burning." The attractive chart of the Caspian Sea is by the Amsterdam publisher Pieter Mortier; in the insets it shows the city of Astrakhan at the mouth of the Volga and the stronghold of Derbent. It was here that Alexander the Great was stopped in his advance north. Disappointed in his attempt, Alexander had a great wall constructed to defend the Persian provinces against the attacks of the Tartars. Because of its strength it was called the "Gate of Iron." Near the left compass rose it is stated that the variance of the compass is 1 degree 44 minutes west.

SOUTH ATLANTIC

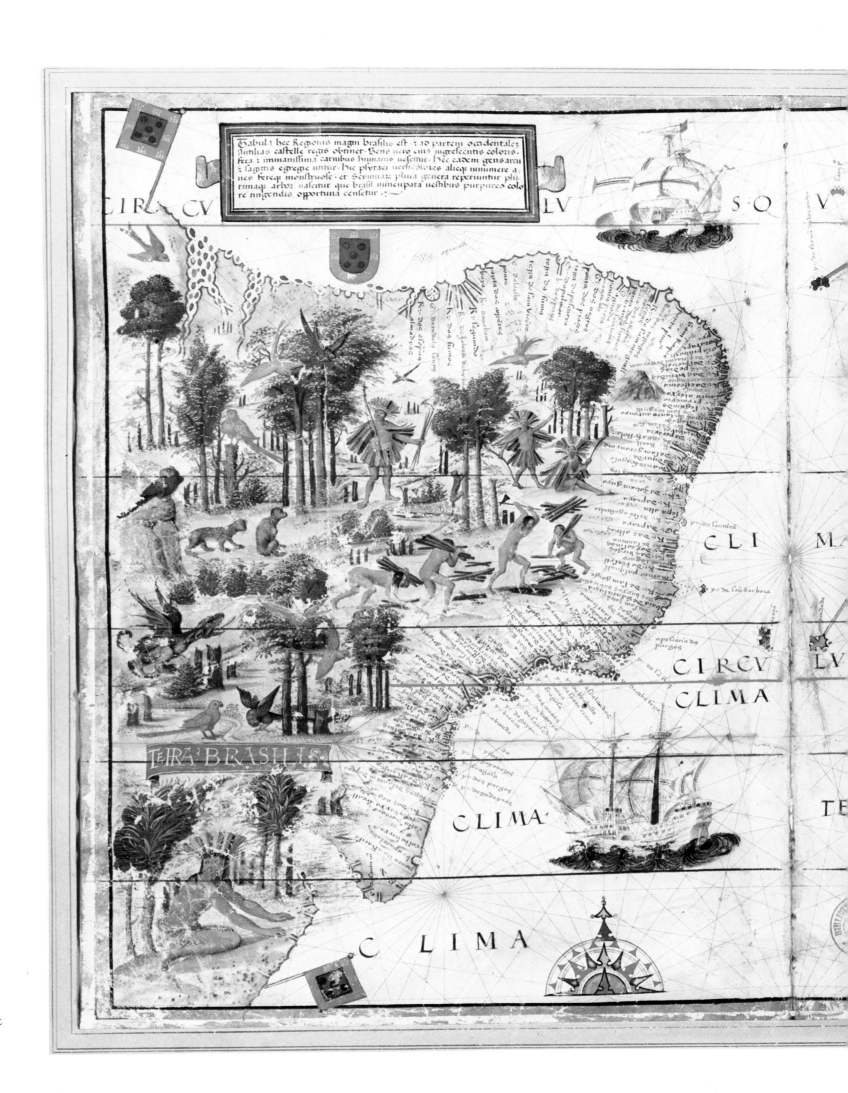

PLATE 10
Portolano of Brazil.
Lopo Homem, Pedro and
Jorge Reinel (Lisbon,
1518–19).
23³⁄₁₆ x 32⁵⁄₁₆″, manuscript
on vellum.
From an untitled atlas.

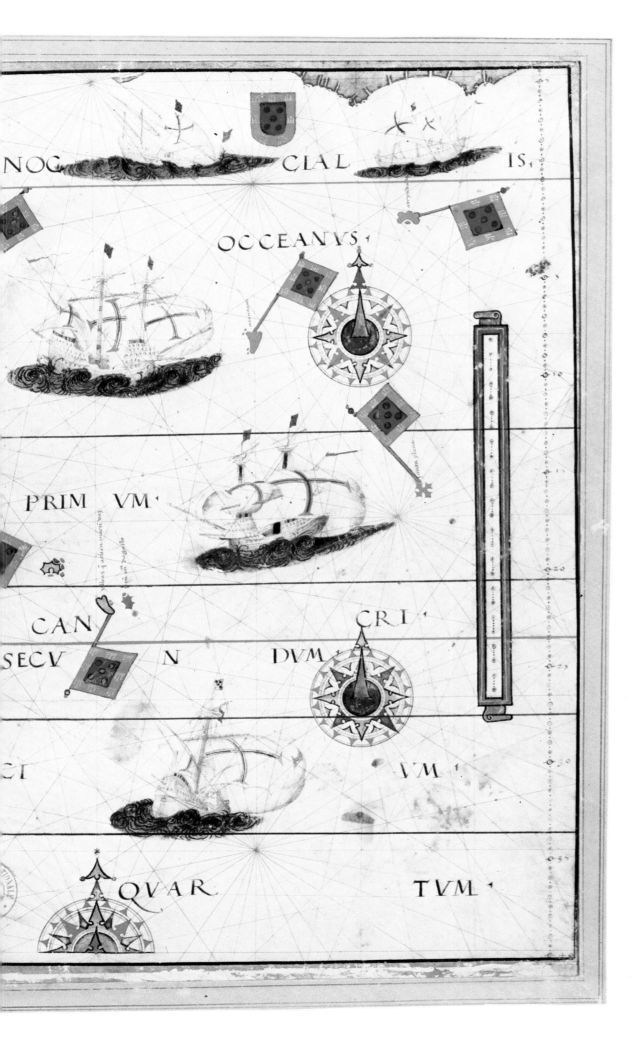

Three months before the official discovery of Brazil by the Portuguese Pedalvarez Cabral, the Spaniard Vincente Yañez Pinzon saw the eastern-most point of the South American continent protruding into the Atlantic Ocean, the cape that afterwards was named Cabo de St. Agostinno. He sailed from there in a northwesterly direction along its coast to the Gulf of Paria, thus becoming the first European to scout the mouth of the Amazon River.

On his way to India around the Cape of Good Hope, Cabral was driven in a westerly direction by currents, and on April 21, 1500, he came upon the Brazilian coast. He took shelter from bad weather in a bay he called Porto Seguro, still the name of a Brazilian port. Cabral erected a great wooden cross and accordingly named the land Santa Cruz. The name was soon changed to Brazil, however, after the abundant red-colored wood that was found there.

By the Treaty of Tordesillas in 1494, the "Raya," or demarcation line, was drawn 370 leagues west of the Cape Verde Islands, dividing the world outside Europe into a Spanish part east of this line and a Portuguese one west of it. As Brazil lay west of this line, it was colonized by the Portuguese, unlike the rest of South America and the West Indies. Amerigo Vespucci surveyed the coast of Brazil for the Portuguese king in two voyages in 1501 and 1503.

This chart belongs to an atlas preserved for centuries in France and traditionally attributed to Pedro and Jorge Reinel. In the 1930s a world map signed by Lopo Homem turned up and appeared to be part of this atlas. The following might be its intriguing history. In 1518–19 the king of Portugal commissioned his cartographer, Lopo Homem, to compile quickly an atlas showing Portuguese discoveries in the world. The beautiful illumination makes it likely that it was to be presented to Francis I of France.

Homem, at that time a young man, probably did not think himself capable of preparing such an atlas alone and tried to engage his teacher, Pedro Reinel. He consented, provided that Homem, who was of high birth, would use his influence at court to secure a pardon for Pedro's son, Jorge. The young Jorge had been forced to flee Lisbon to Seville after a serious fight. The pardon was granted and Pedro Reinel traveled to Seville to return with his son. In Lisbon they prepared the atlas that was to be presented to the royal art-lover Francis I.

When in 1515 the Portuguese Juan Diaz de Solis saw for the first time the immense estuary of the rivers Uruquai, Paraquai, and the Rio de la Plata, he must have hoped that he had discovered the sought-for passage to the Pacific. The chart depicted here, by the hand of an anonymous Portuguese cartographer working around 1538 in the French port of Dieppe, gives an image of these rivers that comes remarkably close to reality. The Uruquai and the Paraquai, with rivers flowing into them, traced to their origins in the interior of Brazil, are more or less correctly depicted.

The wish must have been father to the thought in the image of the same waters in the chart of the southernmost tip of the South American continent made by Guillaume Le Testu in 1555. Here the river has been depicted as a passage to the Pacific. The difference in conception between the two charts is even more remarkable because both cartographers were working in almost the same period and the same place (Dieppe and Le Havre). The French miniaturist, also unknown, gave his fantasies free rein when he illuminated the land with fighting natives in what looks like a French landscape. It does not lessen the decorative character of the chart.

TROPICQVE DE C

PLATE 11
Portolano of the coast of southern Brazil and Rio de la Plata.
Anonymous, School of Dieppe (Dieppe, c. 1538).
16½ x 23¹³⁄₁₆″, manuscript on vellum.
From an untitled atlas.

30

R de plate

Coste du Bresil tirant le detroit de magaillen

RICORNE

Coste du Bresil

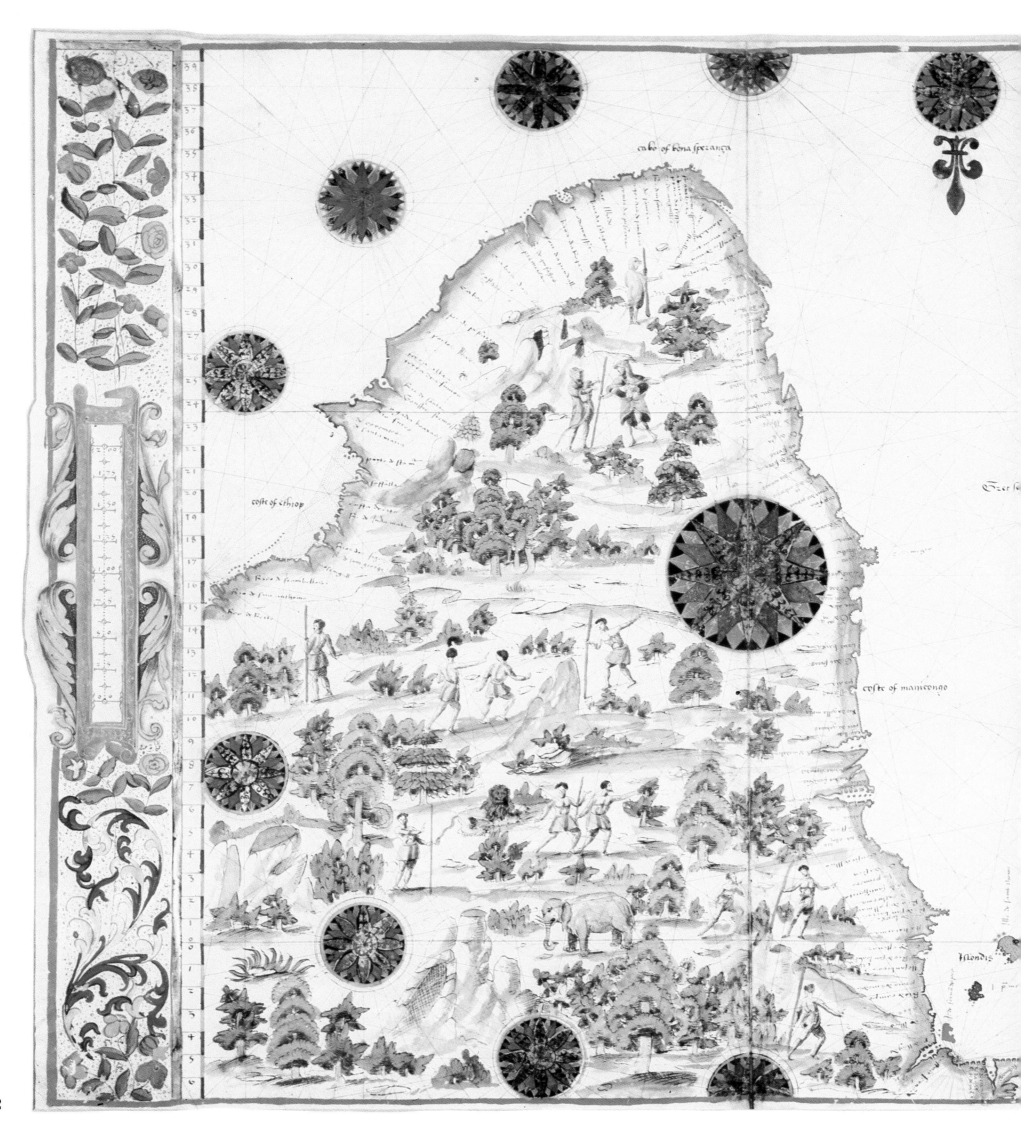

cabo of bona speranca

coste of ethiop

coste of manicongo

Islandis

PLATE 12
Portolano of Southern
Africa.
Jean Rotz (Dieppe and
London, 1542).
28 x 22¼″, manuscript on
vellum.
From the sea atlas *The Boke
of Idrography*.

In the sixteenth century Dieppe was an important center of maritime activity. During their voyages her mariners gathered information that was used by the cartographers of the School of Dieppe. One of these chart makers was Jean Rotz. When he started to work at his world atlas, of which two charts are depicted here, Rotz intended to present it to the French king. But being disappointed in his expectations, he went to England in 1542, where he entered the service of Henry VIII. The English king appointed him hydrographer, and Rotz presented him his atlas. The magnificent portolano atlas with twelve manuscript charts is proof of his abilities as a draughtsman and as an illuminator.

The chart depicted here shows Southern Africa, which was first rounded by Bartholomeu Dias in 1486. The Dutch established a colony at the Cape of Good Hope in 1651, calling it Kaapstad (Cape Town). Here the sick could recover, the ships be repaired, and fresh victuals taken aboard before a long voyage, either to the Indies or back to Europe. Cape Town was taken by the English in 1814.

PLATE 13
View of Table Bay, Cape of
Good Hope.
Johannes Vingboons
(Amsterdam, c. 1650–70).
16½ x 24″, watercolor on
paper.
From the *Vingboons Atlas*, a
collection of charts and
views of harbors outside
Europe.

33

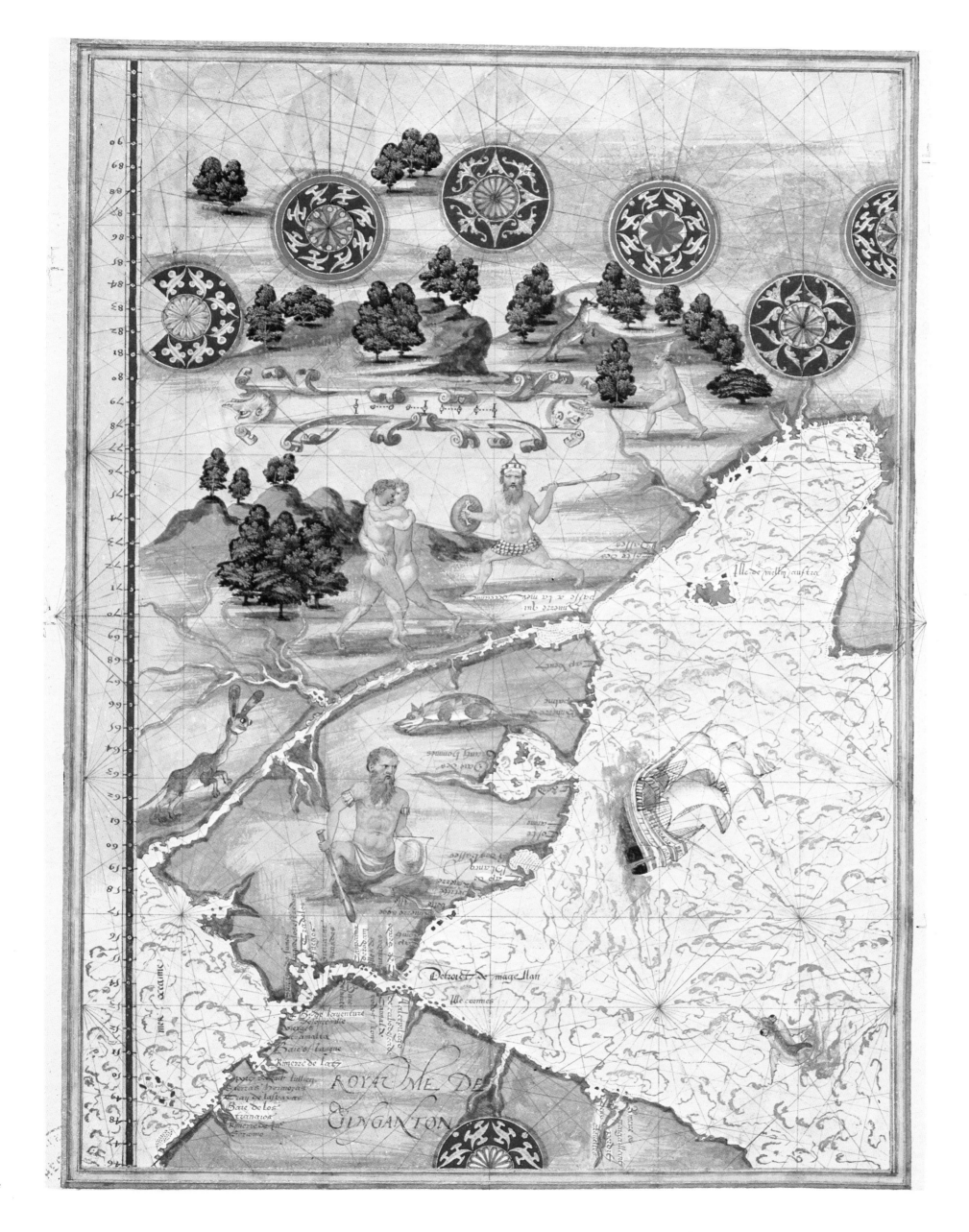

Delroit de magellan

Ule cormes

ROYAUME DE
GINGANTON

Ferdinand Magellan gave his name to the strait in the southern tip of the Americas. He left Spain in 1519, and after reaching the mouth of the Rio de la Plata, discovered by Juan Diaz de Solis in 1515, Magellan sailed south, closely surveying the unknown coasts to find a passage leading to the Pacific. He did not meet any of the inhabitants, but his companions found the imprints of very big feet in the sand, made by natives who wrapped their feet in the skins of animals. Expecting the miraculous in these regions so far away from civilization, the Spanish thought these lands to be inhabited by giants, whom they call "patagonian" or "bigfeet."

On October 24, 1520, they sailed into a bay that proved to be the sought-after passage leading to the Pacific. It took Magellan more than a month to sail through this dangerous strait with its labyrinths of cliffs and bays and its extreme meteorological conditions. He did not see natives in these barren lands either, but at night he did see fires burning on his left and so he named the southern land Tierra del Fuego or "fireland." At last, on November 27, 1520, he reached the Pacific, the first European to do so by ship.

On Garcia Jofre de Loyasa's circumnavigation in 1526, one of his ships sailed through the Strait of Magellan. They reported afterwards that they had seen the end of the continent, but this discovery remained unnoticed. Open water south of the American continent was seen a second time in 1578. On their voyage around the world in that year, Sir Francis Drake's ships entered the Pacific after passing through the Strait of Magellan. Driven south by a fierce storm, Francis Fletcher, commanding one of Drake's ships, saw the tip of the Americas and the open water south of it, but his report was also ignored. The idea that America was connected with the Southland was abandoned only after 1616, when the Dutchmen Willem Schouten and Jacob Lemaire sailed around Cape Horn.

The chart of the Dieppe cartographer Le Testu depicts the southernmost part of the Americas. The Strait of Magellan is shown, and the legend in Magellan's *Tierra del Fuego* reads: *Royaume de Ginganton* (Kingdom of Ginganton). The Rio de la Plata is represented as another passage to the Pacific. On the land giant Patagonians are pictured. The chart is one of the fifty-six charts that make up the atlas *Cosmographie Universelle* made by the Dieppe cartographer Guillaume Le Testu for the French admiral and leader of the French Huguenots, Gaspard de Colignie.

PLATE 15
Quadrant.
From Robert Dudley's *Dell' Arcano del Mare* (Florence, 1646–47).

Le Testu, a Huguenot himself, had participated in expeditions to Brazil, Africa, the East Indies, and perhaps to Australia. The atlas is one of the most extensive sources of hydrographical knowledge at the middle of the sixteenth century. It is also one of the most beautifully executed and decorative atlases of its day.

The charting of a coastline was done while sailing along the coast. By continually taking compass bearings at significant points of that coast and simultaneously measuring the distance sailed between the successive bearings by means of the ship's log, a chart maker can draw in the coastline by triangulation.

In position I an island appears behind Cape A as seen from the ship, a compass bearing is taken, and the ship sails along its course. At the moment Cape A is exactly midship's position II, bearings are taken of the island and Cape F. The ship sails on until Cape F is exactly midship's position III, and bearings are taken again. When the island disappears behind Cape F, the last bearing is taken. The distances covered have been recorded in the ship's log. Starting from the course and the four positions along it, the two capes and the island are located in the chart. Next, the coastline is sketched in the chart. It is evident that the more points of the coast that have been exactly positioned, the more exact becomes the image of the coast in the chart.

PLATE 14
Tierra del Fuego.
Guillaume Le Testu (Le Havre, 1555).
37³⁄₁₆ x 26³⁄₈″, manuscript on vellum.
From an untitled atlas.

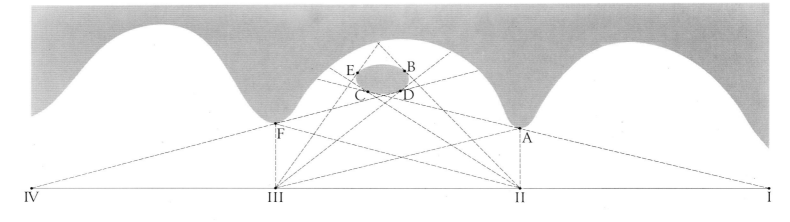

In the second century A.D. the astronomer and mathematician Claudius Ptolemy wrote his famous work, the *Geographia*, in which he discussed the concepts of latitude and longitude: The earth is a globe that is divided by the equator into two equal parts, the Northern and the Southern hemispheres. Latitude circles or parallels are drawn parallel to the equator. Longitude circles, called meridians, are drawn perpendicular to the equator and going to the North and the South poles. One of these meridians is chosen as the prime meridian, and it divides the world into two equal parts, the Western and Eastern hemispheres. In this way an imaginary grid is constructed. Now any place on earth can be defined precisely by its latitude (which is its distance from the equator), and its longitude (its distance from the prime meridian as measured along its parallel).

Ptolemy's *Geographia* was lost during the Middle Ages until a copy of his work and the maps associated with it were found and translated into Latin at the end of the fourteenth century. This discovery gave an enormous impetus to the development of modern geographical sciences and of map making based on scientific concepts.

In the fifteenth century the Portuguese, led by Prince Henry the Navigator, made their first discoveries on the western coast of Africa. After many attempts Cape Bojador was founded in 1434 by Gil Eannes, and in 1460, the year of Prince Henry's death, the Cape Verde Islands were discovered. In these undertakings the Portuguese ventured out of the sight of the coast, and in order to determine their ships' position, they had to depend on astronomical navigation.

PLATE 16
Astrolabe. From Robert
Dudley's *Dell'Arcano del
Mare* (Florence, 1646–47).

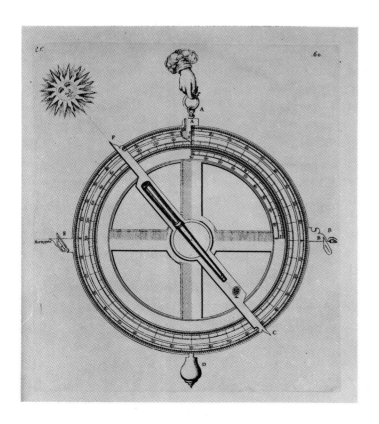

For this they needed reliable methods and instruments to measure the altitude of the sun and the stars from aboard their ships.

Since ancient times mariners had put their trust in the Pole Star, or Polaris, the only fixed star in the skies, which showed them the direction north. The latitude of the observer equals the altitude of Polaris corrected for its distance from the true celestial North Pole. This correction is found by means of Polaris's position in relation to two stars of the constellation Ursa Minor, called the Guards of the North Star. A table, called the Regiment of the North Star, gave these corrections corresponding to the positions of Polaris in relation to its "Guards."

During the fifteenth century several instruments for measuring the altitude of Polaris came into use: the mariner's astrolabe and the Jacob's staff, or cross staff. The astrolabe was known in Europe since its introduction by the Arabs in the tenth century, and in the fifteenth century a modified version came into use. The mariner's astrolabe resembles a four-spoked wheel. It is made of bronze with a jointed ring for holding it and a pivoting arm, called an alidade, with sights through which the heavenly body is observed. From a calibrated scale on the wheel can be read the value of the observed altitude. It was rather awkward to use and not very accurate; at the beginning of the fifteenth century it was superseded by the Jacob's staff.

An instrument for measuring the altitude of the sun or a star, the Jacob's staff is a wooden four-sided shaft, about 30 inches long, on the sides of which scales are calibrated. A crosspiece, or transom, can be moved along the shaft. To use it, the observer pointed the shaft halfway between the sun or star and the horizon and moved the transom along the shaft until its upper end touched the lower side of the sun or the star and its lower end touched the horizon. The altitude of the sun or star could then be read off the scale as given by the transom. The observer aimed the instrument at the sun, hence the term "shooting the sun," in use until recently.

As the Portuguese made progress south along the African coast, they passed the equator, and the Pole Star disappeared behind the horizon. Therefore, they needed another method for computing their latitude. The observer's latitude can also be calculated by observing the sun's altitude at its highest position in the sky, that is, at noon local time. At that time the sun stands in the observer's meridian in the south (in the Northern Hemisphere) or in the north (in the Southern Hemisphere). The latitude of the observer does not equal the sun's altitude with the Pole Star but its complement (90 degrees—the sun's altitude). For the lower the observer's latitude, the higher the sun rises.

To calculate the observer's latitude from the altitude of the sun, the sun's declination must be added or subtracted from its altitude. The declination of the sun varies between 23.3 degrees north at the beginning of the summer in the Northern Hemisphere (approximately June

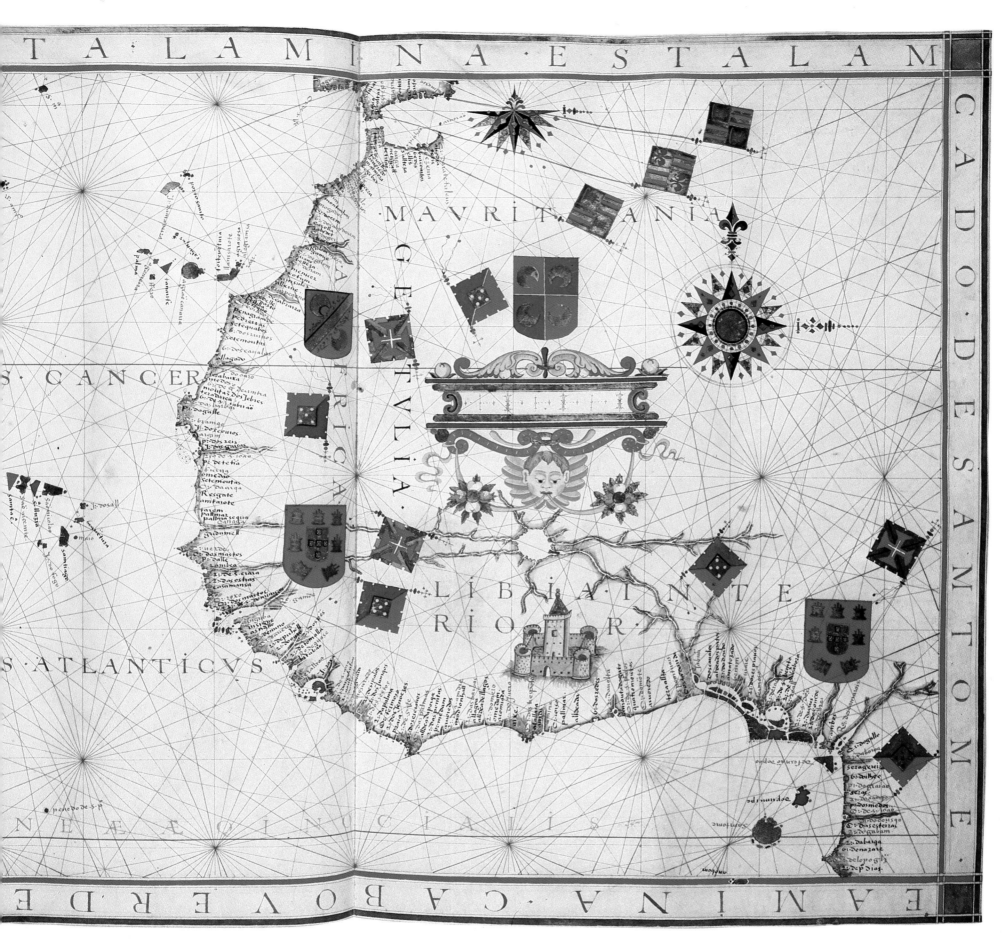

PLATE 17
Portolano of the northern
part of the west coast of
Africa.
Fernao Faz Dourado
(Lisbon, 1575).
15⅜ x 20½″, manuscript on
vellum.
From the atlas *Universalis
Orbis Hydrographia*.

21) and 23.3 degrees south at the beginning of
the winter (approximately December 21).

The sun's declination for all the days of the
year were given in a table, called the Regiment
of the Sun, and was first calculated and used by
the Portuguese at the end of the fifteenth century. By then they had advanced along the coast
of Guinea, reaching Zaire by 1484; in 1486 Bartholomeu Dias rounded the tip of Africa.

Fernao Vaz Dourado is considered to be one of
the most outstanding Portuguese cartographers,
but only six of his atlases, compiled between 1568
and 1580, still survive. He was born in Goa,
India, but received his education in Portugal.
He apparently returned to India, since he was

mentioned as one of the defenders of the Portuguese stronghold of Diu on the Indian coast
during the famous attack in 1546. In 1572 he
returned again to Portugal in the retinue of the
Indian viceroy. He must have longed for the land
of his birth because his last known atlas, bearing the date 1580, was made in Goa, the capital
of the empire and the headquarters of the Portuguese viceroy of India.

The chart depicted here of the waters around
the northwest coast of Africa forms part of an
atlas considered by many the most beautiful of
the six. It was made during Dourado's second
stay in Portugal in 1575 and was dedicated to
King Sebastian.

37

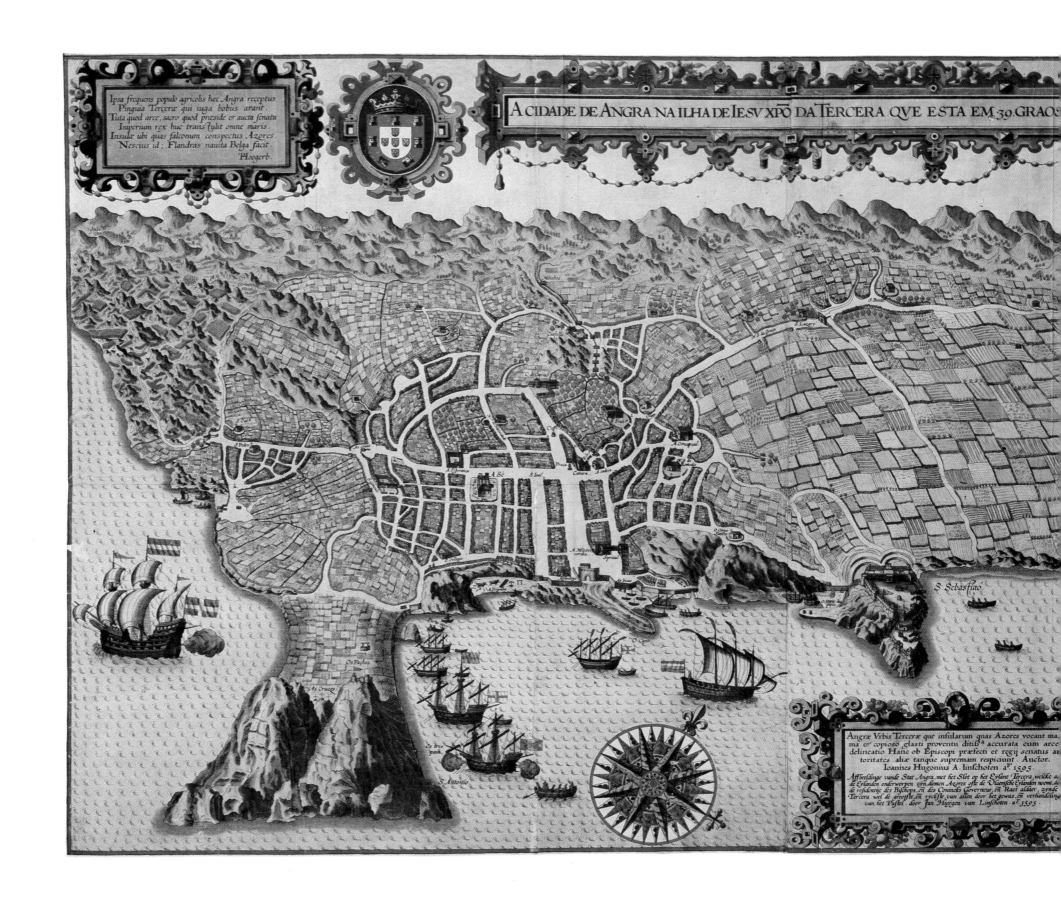

A CIDADE DE ANGRA NA ILHA DE IESV XPO DA TERCERA QVE ESTA EM 39 GRAOS

Born in Haarlem, Jan Huygen van Linschoten (1562/3–1611) was for the greater part of his life a citizen of Enkhuizen, like Jan Lucasz Waghenaer. At the age of sixteen he left for Spain, and five years later he traveled in the suite of the Portuguese archbishop of Goa to Asia. In 1592 he returned to Enkhuizen. The archbishop unintentionally rendered his country a disservice when he took Jan Huygen van Linschoten into his retinue, for the young man was a good listener and a keen observer. The information he gathered proved to be of great value for the Dutch on their first voyages to the East Indies. In 1595 he published the *Reys-Gheschrifte van de Navigatiën der Portugalayiers*, a pilot guide of the Portuguese-dominated Asian seas. His information resulted in his famous *Eerste Schipvaart* to Java. In 1596 he published the *Itenerario*, the account of nineteen years in the service of Spain and Portugal. This book together with the previously published *Reys-Gheeschrifte* described the trading stations of the Portuguese, the sailing routes

PLATE 18
View of the city of Angra on
the island of Terceira.
Jan Huygen van Linschoten
(Amsterdam, 1595).
18⅞ x 32⅞", copper
engraving on paper.
From the *Itenerario*.

To find an alternative to the Spanish- and Portuguese-dominated shipping routes to the East Indies, the English and the Dutch searched the arctic waters for the mythical sea passage to China. A theory, based on vague stories, held that east of Novaja Zeml'a an ice-free passage led past Cape Tabian and through the Strait of Anian to China. In the 1650s the English navigated the western coast of Novaja Zeml'a but did not succeed in finding the passage. The Dutch took over where the English stopped. Huygen participated in the first two voyages of the Dutch in 1594 and 1595 in search of the northeastern passage to China. He advocated the southern passage between the mainland of Asia and Novaja Zeml'a near the island of Waigatsj, contrary to Plancius' notion that the passage north of Novaja Zeml'a should be used since the Kara Sea had no connection with the open passage. The voyages were in vain. (A third voyage led by Willem Barentsz in search of the passage north of Novaja Zeml'a led to his disastrous wintering on Novaja Zeml'a and his death.) After two voyages Jan Huygen van Linschoten remained in Enkhuizen, publishing the account of the voyages made in 1594 and 1595. He died in 1611.

of their eastern navigation, and their commerce in spices and other Asian commodities. It had an enormous influence, being a practical guide for the Dutch expansion in the East Indies. It advised them to concentrate their efforts on Java, as the influence of the Portuguese was felt less there than in the Malaya and Goa areas. For this reason the Dutch were able to push the Portuguese out and establish their commercial empire.

Huygen was never to see the East Indies again.

The charts accompanying van Linschoten's books are by or after Petrus Plancius. His chart of the East Indies remained for decades the prototype for Dutch cartography of the East Indies.

40

Ptolemy compiled his star catalog in the second century A.D. He organized the stars by constellations and positioned each star within the figure of the constellation. The first star maps appeared at the end of the Middle Ages; one of the most famous is Albrecht Dürer's flat star map of 1515. As in a terrestrial map, a system of coordinates of latitude north or south and of longitude east or west is applied; in a celestial map either an ecliptical coordination system or a celestial equatorial system of coordinates is used.

The first system is based upon the apparent annual path of the sun: the ecliptic.

In this system, celestial latitude is the angular distance north or south of the ecliptic, while celestial longitude is the distance along the ecliptic from the vernal equinox (the position of the sun at the beginning of spring in the Western Hemisphere). By this system all stars can be unambiguously positioned. A flat chart based on this system is a planispheric projection map in the form of a circle with the northern or southern ecliptic pole as the center.

In the celestial equatorial system the coordinates "declination" and "right ascension" are used. The declination is the angular distance from the celestial equator, measured along the hour circle. The right ascension is the distance along the celestial equator measured from the vernal equinox to the point of intersection of the hour circle going through the star and the celestial equator.

The hour circle going through the vernal equinox, the celestial poles, and the autumnal equinox have the same function in this system as the prime meridian (of Greenwich) in the system of coordinates on the earth. A flat star map based on this system is a planispheric projection map in the form of a circle with the north or south celestial pole as center.

Stars and constellations of stars are pinpointed by their coordinates. When one knows a certain star's declination and right ascension, one knows in advance the approximate position of a star needed for astronomical position-finding at sea

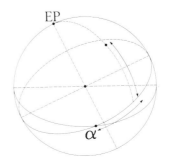
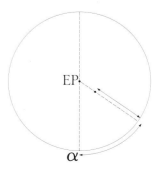

by means of "shooting" stars with the Jacob's staff or, in later times, with the sextant. Ptolemy used the ecliptic coordinates; in modern astronomy the celestial equatorial coordinate system superseded Ptolemy's system.

In the sixteenth century the astronomer Tycho Brahe enlarged the Ptolemic catalog of Northern stars by his observations on the Danish island of Sven, while at the end of the century a catalog of Southern stars was compiled by the Dutch navigators Pieter Dirkz Keyser and Cornelis de Houtman on their first voyages to the Indian seas.

In the Southern Hemisphere the Southern Cross replaced the Pole Star as the means for finding latitude. The two star maps depicted, giving the constellations of stars of the Northern and Southern Hemispheres, are from Andreas Cellarius's celestial atlas entitled *Harmonia Macrocosmica*, the only celestial atlas produced in the Netherlands. The identity of the author is obscure, and no other works by his hand are known. The publisher was the well-known Johannes Janssonius, the lifetime rival of the publishing house of the Blaeus. He incorporated the celestial atlas as Part XI of his *Atlas Mayor*, published in 1658.

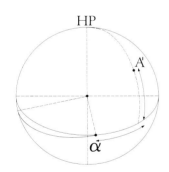
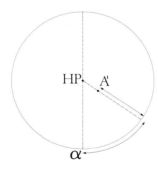

PLATE 20
Celestial map of the Southern Hemisphere. Andreas Cellarius and Johannes Janssonius (Amsterdam, 1660). 17⁵⁄₁₆ x 20¹⁄₁₆", copper engraving on paper. From the *Atlas Coelestis, seu Harmonia Macrocosmica*.

42

STELLATUM
ANTIQUUM.

43

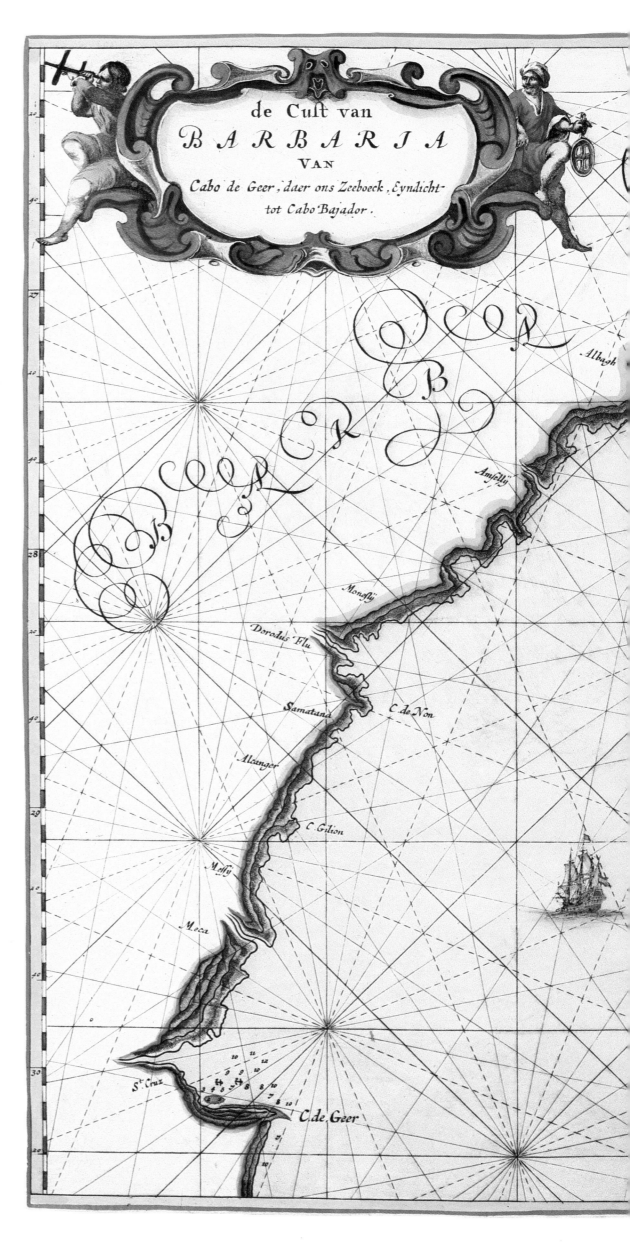

The sea chart from the atlas issued in 1676 by the Amsterdam publisher Hendrik Goos depicts the coasts of Morocco and Fuerteventura and Lanzarote, two of the Canary Islands that lie on the route to the West as well as the East Indies. Ships stopped there for provisioning, and afterwards the voyage continued either to the West Indies or to the coast of Brazil and then to the Cape of Good Hope.

On the chart Cape Bojador is just visible; it was first rounded in 1434 by the Portuguese mariner Gil Eannes.

In the chart, rhumb lines are drawn starting from the compass roses, as are latitude and longitude lines. In the borders a scale of latitude degrees is given. For large-scale charts of moderate latitude the fault of the plane chart can be neglected. For depicting large areas or areas close to the poles, however, the plane chart cannot be used.

In the cartouche at the right the numbers of German, Spanish, French, and English miles in one degree are given; the use of so many different mileage systems caused much confusion at the time.

44

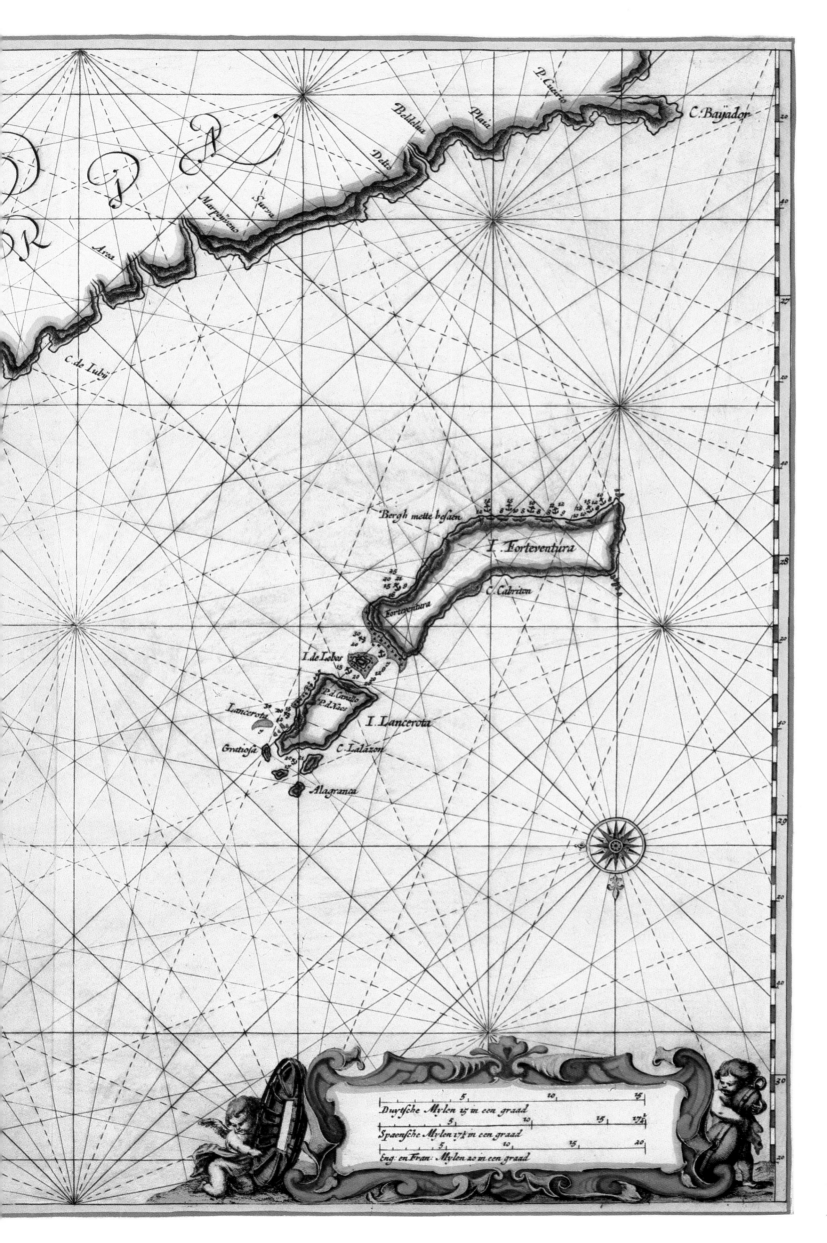

P. Cesrino

C. Bayador

Beldolut

Plata

Dolta

Starro

Murrogieno

Area

C. de Iuby

Bergh mette befaen

I. Forteventura

C. Cabrutza

Forteventura

I. de Lobas

P. d. Gerollo o p. d. Naes

Lancerota

I. Lancerota

Gratiofa

C. Lalazon

Alagranca

Duytsche Mylen 15 in een graad

5   10   15

Spaensche Mylen 17½ in een graad

5   10   15   17½

Eng: en Fran: Mylen 20 in een graad

5   10   15   20

PLATE 21
Sea chart of the coast of
Morocco and two of the
Canary Islands.
Hendrik Goos (Amsterdam,
1676).
16¹⁵⁄₁₆ x 19¹¹⁄₁₆″, copper
engraving on paper.
From the atlas *The Sea
Atlas of the Water World.*

45

WEST INDIES

Christopher Columbus's voyage of discovery was based on an error made thirteen centuries earlier. Ptolemy, the geographer of antiquity, grossly underestimated the unknown world in the west. In his thinking there was no continent between Europe and Southeast Asia. Medieval geographers thought the distance between the Canary Islands and China to be less than 90 degrees—in reality it is about 220 degrees, or 13,200 nautical miles. When Columbus made his landfall on October 12, 1492, on Watling—one of the Bahamas—he mistook it for an island in the vicinity of Japan; he died believing that he had reached Asia.

After Columbus's first voyage, a host of adventurers, attracted by the stories of immense treasures, tried their luck. After sixty years of daring expeditions, incredible treasures, and unnameable sufferings, the conquest of the Spanish Americas had been completed, and one of the most turbulent chapters of history ended.

On his first voyage Columbus also discovered Cuba and Haiti, which he named Hispaniola, or "little Spain." His second voyage brought him to the Lesser Antilles, which he scouted. He also discovered Jamaica and sailed along Cuba's south coast, but due to the condition of his ships he had to return before he discovered it to be an island. On his third and fourth voyages he discovered Trinidad, the Gulf of Paria, and Margarita, where he found pearls in abundant quantities; he sailed along the coast of Honduras to the Isthmus of Darien, where he heard about a sea on the other side of the Isthmus but mistook it for the Gulf of Bengal.

In the meantime, several other voyages of exploration were made. Alvonso de Jojedo, Juan de la Cosa (Columbus's pilot), Per Alonso Niño, Vincente Yañez Pinto, and the Florentine Amerigo Vespucci surveyed the northwest coast of South America around the turn of the century.

A caprice of history robbed Christopher Columbus of the honor of giving his name to the New World. Amerigo Vespucci popularized the knowledge of the New World, exaggerating his own part in its discovery. For this reason the outstanding geographer Martin Waldseemuller first gave the name "America" to the New World in the 1515 edition of Ptolemy's atlas; others followed, and the name "America" stuck.

The Spanish cartography of the New World was organized by the *Casa para la Contraction y Negociacon de los Indias*, or "bureau of the Indies

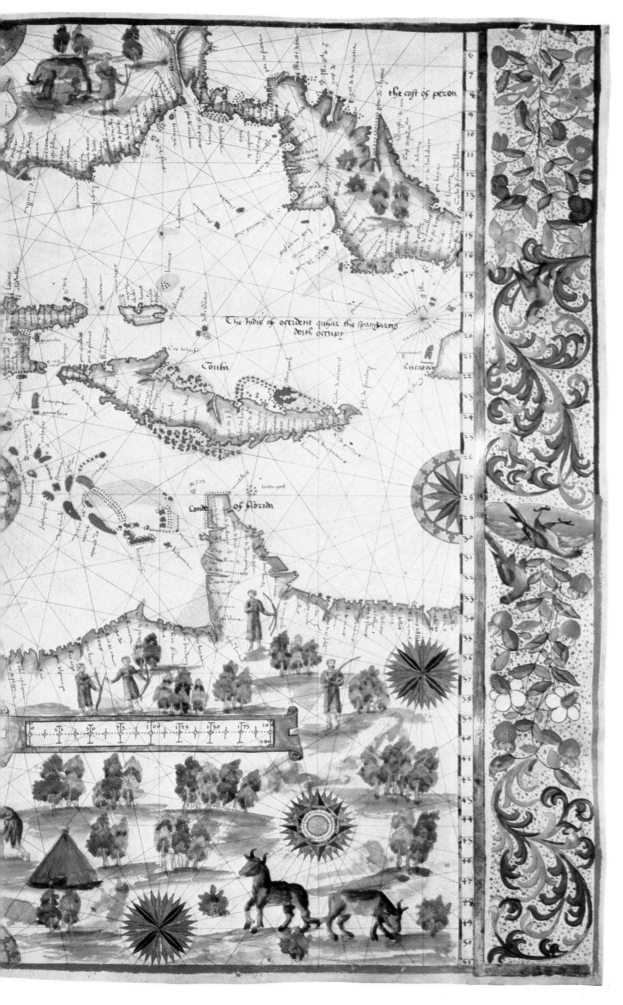

The coſt of pezon

The Indis of occident qukuz the ſpanyzarnzg doith occiupy

Couba

Cucatan

Conde of floridn

trade," established at Seville in 1503. In 1508 this bureau appointed Amerigo Vespucci as "Pilot Mayer" with the order to draw a royal *padron general*, or master chart, and to keep it up-to-date. This master chart, continually amended and corrected for the latest discoveries, formed the prototype for all Spanish charts of the Americas. After his death in 1512, Vespucci was succeeded in this office by Juan Diaz de Solis and after his death at Rio de la Plata by Sebastian Cabot.

The surveying of the coasts of the West Indies was continued by Francisco Hernandez de Cordova who sailed along a part of the coast of the Yucatan peninsula. The following year Juan de Grijalva surveyed the Mexican coast from Yucatan to present-day Tampico. Both were told stories of great cities with fabulous riches; these stories led to the conquest of Mexico by Hernando Cortes.

In 1519 the last unknown parts of the coast of the Gulf of Mexico from Tampico to Florida, discovered by Ponce de Leon in 1512, were surveyed by Alonso de Piñeda, making it clear that there was no water passage to the Pacific in that part of the Americas.

Jean Rotz, the maker of this beautiful portolano chart of the Caribbean, was court hydrographer to the English king Henry VIII, to whom he presented the atlas of which this chart forms a part. With its beautifully illuminated borders, it is a fine example of Tudor chartmaking.

PLATE 22
Portolano of the Caribbean.
Jean Rotz (Dieppe and
London, 1542).
22¼ x 28″, manuscript on
vellum.
From the sea atlas *The
Boke of Idrography*.

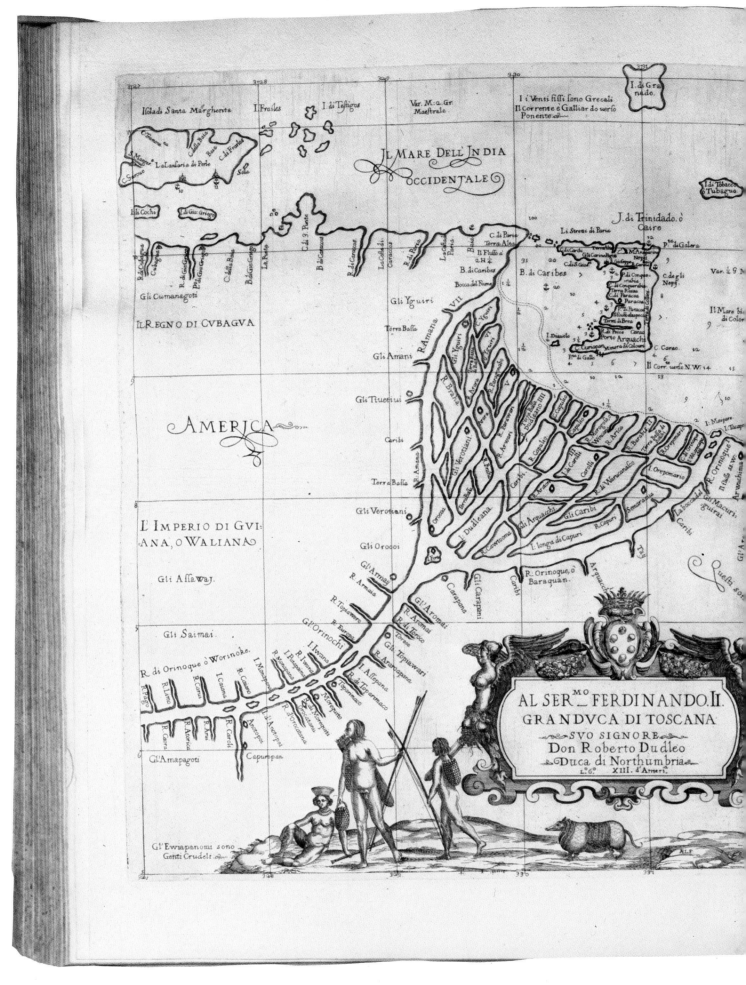

Sir Robert Dudley (1574–1649) was born the illegitimate son of Queen Elizabeth's favorite, the earl of Leicester. In 1594 he led an expedition to Guyana. He lost favor at court and had to flee England. He settled in Florence and served the Medici for the rest of his life. He was an accomplished shipbuilder and an authority on naval warfare, but his magnum opus is the sea atlas *Dell' Arcano del Mare* ("The Secrets of the Sea"), published in 1648–49 shortly before his death.

This atlas is remarkable for several reasons. It is the first printed sea atlas with charts covering the whole world, and all the charts, including detailed ones of coastal areas, are based upon the Mercator projection method. Longitude and latitude lines are drawn, but there are no rhumb lines, which was unusual for that time.

One wonders whether such an atlas was ever actually used aboard a ship—despite its royal presentation—since it deviated so much from the customary sea charts of those times. Nonetheless Dudley made an outstanding contribution to cartography with the publication of his *Arcano del Mare*, not least because of its beautiful engrav-

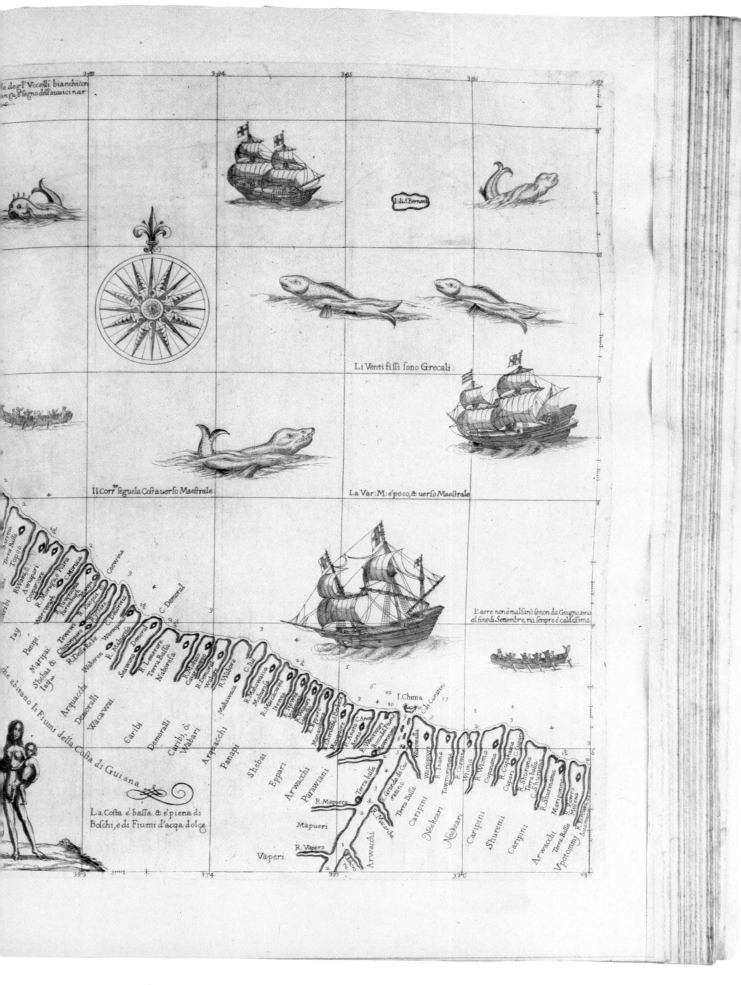

PLATE 23
Sea chart of the coast of
Guyana.
Robert Dudley (Florence,
1648).
18⅛ x 28⅜″, copper
engraving on paper.
From the sea atlas *Dell'-
Arcano del Mare*.

ing and calligraphy by the Italian engraver Antonio Francisco Lucini. The introduction to the atlas states that Lucini spent twelve years engraving the plates, and used 5,000 pounds of copper in the process.

The chart from Dudley's atlas depicted here must be based upon material gathered during his own expedition to Guyana in 1594 and that of Raleigh in 1595. These expeditions were encouraged by the legend of El Dorado, the Golden One, a vast empire or city with fabulous riches in the interior of Guyana. The English sailed up the river Orinoco in search of the city of Manao, said to be situated at the border of a great salt lake, Parime, which the Spaniards had previously failed to find.

Raleigh reached the mouth of the Caroni but, forced back because of the river's rising water, he never had a glimpse of the magical city. He had heard stories about a nation that he held to be true: "a nation of people . . . have their eyes in their shoulders and their mouths in the middle of their breasts and that a long train of hair groweth backwards between their shoulders."

DE STADT ENDE BAY VAN HAVANA

GLEEGEN OP 'T EYLANDT CVBA.

PLATE 24
View of Havana.
Johannes Vingboons
(Amsterdam, c. 1650–70).
16½ x 21¼″, watercolor on
paper.
From the *Vingboons Atlas*, a
collection of charts and
views of harbors outside
Europe.

There exists in The Hague a collection of manuscript sea charts and views of ports outside Europe called the *Vingboons Atlas* after its maker Johannes Vingboons (1617–1670). Vingboons worked for the great Amsterdam publisher Johannes Blaeu. Johannes, like his father, Willem, was chief cartographer to the Dutch East Indies Company and was responsible for the amending and correcting of the so-called "secret atlas" of the company, which consisted of sea charts and views of the harbors beyond Europe.

In the 1760s Johannes worked at the enlarging of his *Atlas Mayor*, already composed of twelve parts. This project has been called the most ambitious project of publication ever thought of, for Blaeu intended to publish charts and maps of all the lands, seas, and heavens. He wanted to publish a sea atlas of the Eastern and Western hemispheres as a part of his *Atlas Mayor* and in 1665 entered in negotiations with the Lords XVII, the directors of the East Indies Company. The "secret atlas" at that time was not very secret any more and the Lords considered the publication of a printed atlas of the Indian waters. But, due to financial reasons, the negotiations came to nothing, which displeased Blaeu who had the manuscript material already at his disposal.

The views depicted give an impression of the quality of the unpublished sea atlas. This one, in particular, shows seventeenth-century Havana with its fortresses defending its harbor.

51

NACHT   WYSER

PLATE 25
Sea chart of Cuba and
Jamaica.
Arent Roggeveen and Pieter
Goos (Amsterdam, 1675).
16⁵⁄₁₆ x 20⁷⁄₈″, copper
engraving on paper.
From the sea atlas *The
Burning Fen, Part One.*

52

If in the beginning Spanish discoveries were financially disappointing—Columbus's first voyages did not cover their costs—that soon changed. Starting with pearls from the island of Margarita, a trickle of precious metals and stones soon grew to a stream counted in tons. At the start, the Spanish galleons made their return voyages alone. But their valuable cargo attracted privateers from all nations, licensed and unlicensed, attacking from the West Indies to the mouth of the Guadalquivir in Spain. Soon it became obligatory to sail in convoys, the famous armadas. From the end of the sixteenth century, when the Spanish American vice-royalties of New Spain, Tierra Firma, and Peru were formed, a system of convoy sailing was established that did not change much for over two centuries. All armadas sailed from Spain down the African coast to the Canary Islands. After refitting, the ships sailed in a westerly direction, favored by the equatorial currents and the trade winds, to the Lesser Antilles, from which they continued their voyage either to Cartagena on the Colombian coast or to Vera Cruz in Mexico. The return voyage started from Havana, through the channel between Florida and the Bahamas with the Gulf Stream and the Westerlies, and passed east of Bermuda to the Azores and from there to Spain.

The voyage out and the return generally took seven to nine months. Each year in spring the New Spain Armada departed from Spain, and after reaching the Lesser Antilles, it continued south of Hispaniola and Cuba to Vera Cruz on

the Mexican coast where it unloaded its cargo. Then it reloaded with products from Mexico and Honduras, including silver from Mexican mines.

At the end of each summer the Tierra Firma Armada sailed from Seville to the West Indies. The fleet sailed through the Lesser Antilles, along the coasts of Venezuela and Colombia to Cartagena. A message was sent to Callao on the Peruvian coast, and upon its arrival, the South Sea Armada weighed anchor and sailed to Panama. Here the cargo was unloaded and carried across the Isthmus to Portobello where the Tierra Firma lay waiting to load pearls, emeralds, gold, and silver—and the platinum that the Spaniards valued less and called "false silver."

The armadas were always accompanied by two fighting galleons, the *capitano* at the head of the fleet with the general in command, and the *almirante* closing the rear with the admiral, who took command during battle. The warships, with more armament and marines than the freighters, always carried precious metals in huge quantities, often using the gold and silver ingots as ballast. These galleons were the most sought-after prizes.

In Roggeveen's chart of the islands of Cuba and Jamaica, north is down, as indicated by the "fleur-de-lys" of the compass-rose. The chart here depicted forms a part of the "Burning Fen," the pilot-guide by Arent Roggeveen and published by Pieter Goos in 1675. The chart shows the coasts of Honduras and the peninsula of Yucatan.

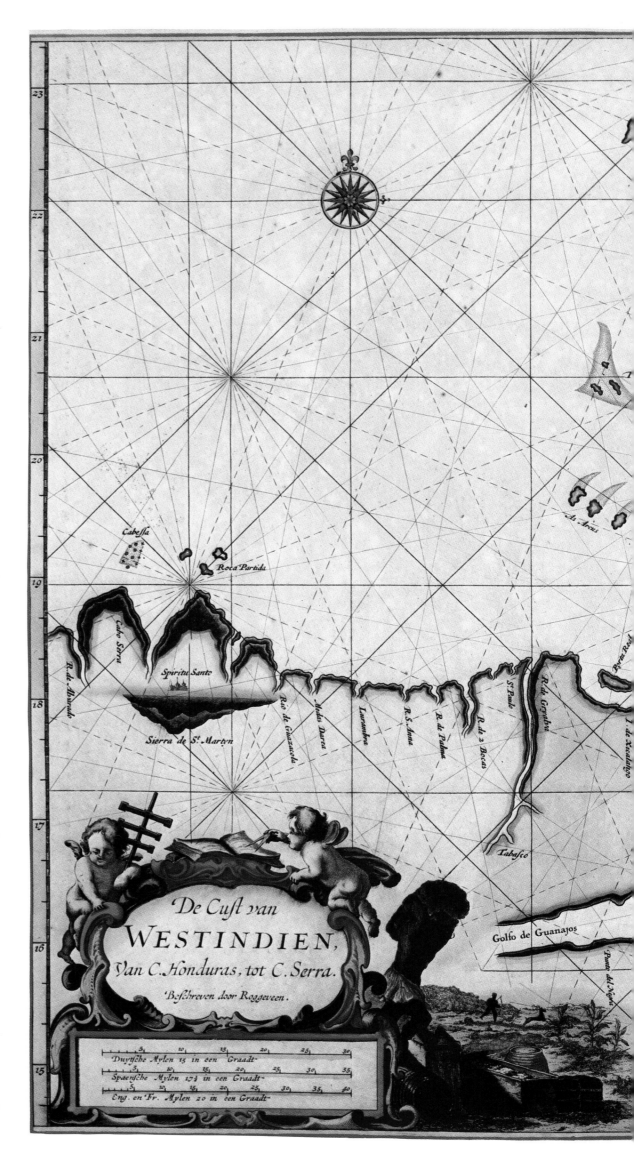

54

PLATE 26
Sea chart of the Yucatan
peninsula.
Arent Roggeveen and Pieter
Goos (Amsterdam, 1675).
15¹⁵⁄₁₆ x 20¹⁄₁₆″, copper
engraving on paper.
From the sea atlas *The
Burning Fen, Part One.*

55

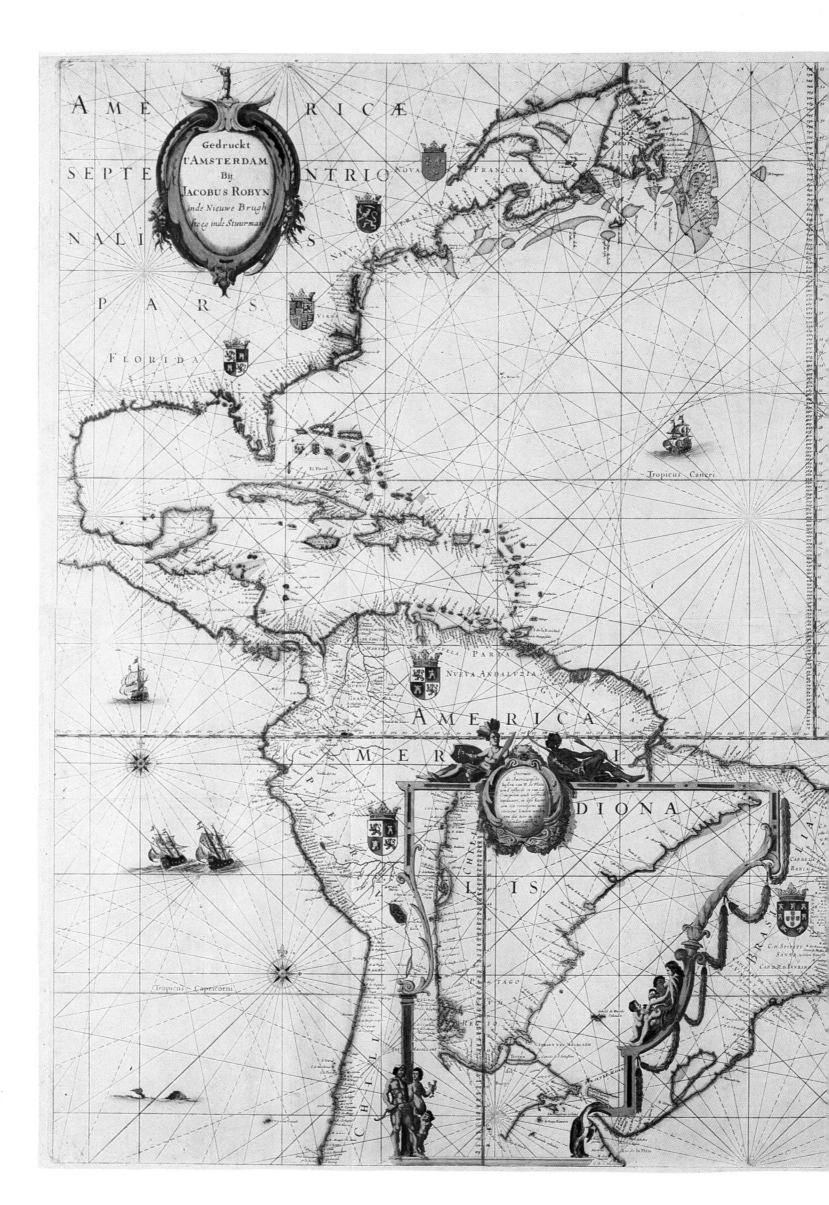

PLATE 27
Sea chart of the West Indies
and the Atlantic Ocean.
Willem Jansz Blaeu and
Jacob Robijn (Amsterdam,
1625–30/1685–90).
32¹⁄₁₆ x 39″, copper
engraving on paper.

56

We have seen before that a ship's position can be determined when its latitude and longitude are known. The Portuguese developed methods and instruments to determine their ships' latitude during their years of exploration along the African coasts. These exploits were in a southerly direction. The Spanish expeditions, however, sailed to the west, and when they made a landfall, it was important to know the exact longitude.

Theoretically, determining longitude is quite simple. When an observer knows what the time is at the chosen prime meridian when the local time is 12 noon (that is, the moment the sun stands in the observer's highest position in the sky, or the moment the sun stands in the meridian or longitude circle of the observer), the difference in local time and prime meridian time equals the value of the longitude of the observer's position. In the sixteenth century the meridian of the Azores was generally chosen as the prime meridian, although several other meridians were used as well. The Greenwich meridian has been accepted by all nations as the prime meridian.

The practical application on board was as difficult as the theory is simple. Gemma Frisius, the Dutch mathematician who introduced the theory in 1530, suggested the use of a clock. It took nearly 250 years to construct a clock that met the requirements of exactness. The Englishman John Harrison (1693–1776) solved the problem when he constructed his famous chronometers.

In the meantime, other methods of determining longitude were tried and found invalid. One method was based on the differences in the variation of the magnetic compass. The variation or declination of the compass needle is caused by the magnetic field of the earth, and its value differs for different places on the earth. Some mathematicians thought that differing variations could be used to determine the longitude of a particular place. For this an instrument

57

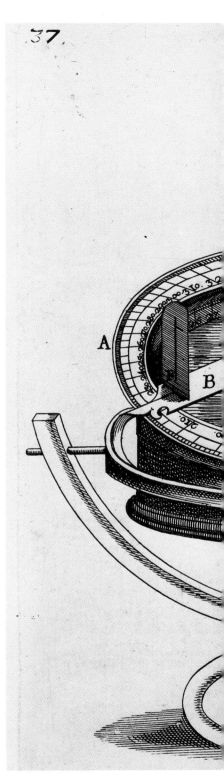

called an *astrolabium catholicum* was used. The theory on which the method was based, however, proved to be wrong. The mariner had to be content with the method of dead reckoning at sea: when out of sight of the coast, find position by measuring the angles of the compass-needle with the directions sailed and the distances covered by means of the log. The method only piles error upon error and was infamous for its inaccuracy. Yet it was popular among mariners for a long time because the simple seaman could understand what was being done, unlike astronomical navigation and the theory on which it is based—something of which the mariner in general understood little. In fact, he learned the use of these methods only by rote.

The method of dead reckoning is simple: The seaman kept a record of the consecutive courses steered, the distances covered, and the corresponding time lapses from the point and time of departure, and he was thus able to plot his track on the chart. A simple instrument, called a traverse board, could be used.

The method is still in use today, and it is useful provided that it is corrected daily by astronomical observations. When the exact position is determined, the record of courses held and distances covered is started again and then corrected again.

Formerly, only the latitude of the ship could be determined by means of the mariner's astrolabe or the Jacob's staff. As the astronomical instruments were not very accurate and the average mariner understood little of the methods employed, the seaman clung to the approved method of dead reckoning. The exactness of the method depended on the exactness by which the angle, the distance, and the corresponding time lapses were measured. Time keeping on board was a grave problem and a "human factor" was added. Time keeping depended on the correct use of the hourglass, but seamen often turned the glass before it was completely empty in order to shorten their watch. This was called "sand

eating." The result was that the distance covered was overestimated. The speed through the water was measured by means of the hand log and a small log glass. The log consisted of a triangular piece of wood attached to the log line, which was knotted at regular intervals. The duration of the log glass and the linear measure used determined the length of the intervals between the knots. The log line, with the log at the end, was played out astern, the sand glass was turned, and the number of knots played out were counted until the sand glass was empty. The number of knots counted gave the speed of the ship through the water, but the distance thus measured had to be corrected for the influence of the water currents. These corrections were only estimates, however.

The angle between the compass needle, seeking north, and the so-called "lubber's line" of the compass, which indicates the ship's axis fore and aft, gives the direction sailed. But corrections nearly always have to be made before a course can be plotted on a chart. First of all, the lubber's line indicates the movement of the ship through the water and has to be corrected for currents that cause the ship to drift.

The compass needle does not always indicate a true northerly direction. First, a so-called "deviation" of the compass is caused by the magnetic field of the ship. Its value differs with the ship's course. Therefore, the value of the deviation must be ascertained for each point of the compass. This is done by "swinging the ship," that is, comparing the compass bearings of the sun with its known correct bearing at that time while the ship completes a full turn of 360 degrees. For this an alidade, a pivoting arm with two sights, is attached to the top of the compass. After correcting for the deviation, another calculation must be made before a "deviation scale" can be devised. This calculation corrects for the variation or declination, which is caused by earth's magnetic field, the value of which differs for different places on the globe. When sailing

PLATE 28
Compass with alidade. From Robert Dudley's *Dell' Arcano del Mare* (Florence, 1646–47).

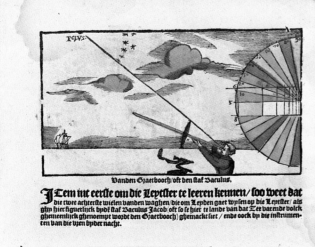

PLATE 29
Jacob's or cross staff. From Govaert Willemsen van Hollesloot's *Die Caerte vande Oost ende West Zee* (Harlingen, 1588).

from the Mediterranean westward, as Columbus did, it changes from east to zero on the longitude of the Azores to west in American seas. As this phenomenon was unknown before the voyages to the Americas were undertaken, it deceived the early cartographers into drawing the eastern coastline of the Americas in a nearly east-west direction.

Comparing the true north direction with the magnetic north direction gives the sum of deviation and variation. Having previously computed the deviation for the ship's course, the variation can be calculated.

The chart shown of the Atlantic Ocean (plate 27) is a small-scale cross-over, based upon the Mercator projection. The printed chart was meant to be used especially for the navigation to West Africa and the Americas. Together no less than eight Dutch publishers issued twelve editions of this chart over a period of almost a century. In this period mariners used this chart for navigating in the Atlantic. The first edition was made by the Dutch cartographer Willem Blaeu and issued between 1625 and 1630. Later editions are by Jacob Colom, Antoniesz Lootsman, Hendrik Doncker, Pieter Goos, Johannes van Keulen, Jacob Robijn, and Johannes Loots. This copy was issued by Jacob Robijn between 1685 and 1690. In the chart, Staten Land in the southern tip of the Americas is not replaced by Staten Island, despite the fact that Hendrik Brouwer in 1643 had discovered it to be an island.

Although the coasts are not always positioned correctly in the chart—longitude is often especially at fault—at the time it was first used, the chart was a progressive hydrographical work, and compared with the plane chart normally used then, it was an enormous step forward.

Jacob Robijn started selling charts in 1673. After a short association with Johannes van Keulen—afterwards his rival—he acquired the plates of Goos's *Zeespiegel* and *Zee Atlas* after 1680 and republished these pilot guides of the seas of Europe, West Africa, and America.

WESTERN EUROPEAN WATERS

During the second half of the sixteenth century, rutters and compass charts—in manuscript and printed form—provided mariners with a considerable amount of information about European coastal areas. Even so, when Lucas Weghenaer's publication *Spieghel der Zeevaerdt* (*Mariner's Mirror*) appeared on the market in 1584, it marked a turning point in the development of nautical charts and pilot guides. In many ways a unique hydrographical work, for several reasons, the *Spieghel* served as a model for all seventeenth-century pilot guides and sea atlases.

It was the first printed volume of its kind to contain a systematically compiled collection of compass charts and sailing directions giving the mariner all the necessary information for voyages along the western European coasts. Secondly, the *Spieghel der Zeevaerdt* standardized symbols for navigational aids such as buoys, beacons, and landmarks, as well as the presentation of information about channels, harbors, and anchorages. Depths were given in fathoms indicating the tidal date (half-flood or ebb).

In addition, with two exceptions (Mercator's *World Chart* of 1569 and Diego Homem's *Chart of the Mediterranean* of 1579), all such charts had previously been printed from woodblocks, but Waghenaer's charts were all printed from copperplates, a superior medium for the reproduction of hydrographical information. Hence, the introduction of these charts made all earlier charts printed from woodblocks obsolete.

The folio format of the *Spieghel der Zeevaerdt* also became standard for all Dutch pilot guides during the seventeenth century. Likewise, this publication set the precedent of grouping the northern and eastern navigation with pertinent charts and sailing directions from the coast of Holland to the coasts of North Russia and the Baltic separately from the western navigation with its charts and sailing directions for the coasts of England and the Channel coast south to the Cape Verde Islands. A later guide to the Mediterranean issued by William Barentsz in 1595 was incorporated as the third part of the *Spieghel der Zeevaerdt*, a convention main-

PLATE 30
Sea chart of the coast of Southwest England. Lucas Jansz Waghenaer (Enkhuizen, 1584). 13 x 20 1/16", copper engraving on paper. From the pilot guide *The Mariner's Mirror*.

Opdoenninghe vande Sorlinges, als die oost noort oost
van v. syn twe mylen.

De Sorlinges als die zuydt oost van v. syn
omtrent twe mylen.

Engelants eyndt, soet hem verthoont
comende wth de Spaensche Zee.

Tlandt bij oosten, engelants
eyndt, alst drie mylen
oost noort oost va v. is.

Lijsaert, alst west eyndt,
noort west van v. leyt een myl
en oost eyndt Noorden twe mylen.

Vaelmuyen, alst Slot noort west ten westen
van v. leyt, en Doedemans hooft drie
mylen Noorden van v. is.

men hem de Landen van Lijsaert, Vaelmuyen, enn Doedemans hooft, alst Slot noort west, ten westen van v. is, omtrent
twe mylen, en Doedemans hooft mede noerden van v. is drie mylen.

Vaelmuyen.

S. Gorsmayn.

Doedemans hooft.

Taunstock.

shol.

Treuring.

A N G L I Æ   P A R S.

Plejmondt.

Slot

S. Michil.

Vaelmuyen.

Peryn

tEylandt.

Warkaio

Gentelmans hoys.

Menog.

Hilforde.

Mause.

Fanvyck.

Saltaske.

Fouu.

Saltesleu.

Ramshooft.

Lourve.

De nijew steen.

Coex broot.

Banck

Tringy

Doetmans
hooft.

thooft.

SEPTENTRIO.

OCCIDENS

tusschen Engelandt ende Vranck ryck

ORIENS

MERIDIES.

Cum Priuilegio
ad decenniu.
1.5.8

Spaensche mylen tot 17½. in een graedt.

Duytsche mylen tot 15. in een graedt.

tained throughout the seventeenth and eighteenth centuries.

Born around 1534, Lucas Jansz Waghenaer spent most of his life in Enkhuizen on the Zuiderzee (now the fresh-water lake Ijsselmeer). At that time, the city was one of The Netherlands' most important trading centers. Waghenaer began his career as a pilot, but later, in 1579, he decided to stay ashore to prepare his first pilot guide. Undoubtedly, much of its information was based on his own seafaring experience.

Since he was not a man of means, he was constantly busy raising funds to cover the heavy financial burden incurred in connection with cutting the copperplates used to print his charts. The problem was eliminated to some extent when the *Spieghel der Zeevaerdt* was printed by the famous publishing house of Plantijn in Leiden and proved to be a success, both in Holland and elsewhere.

In 1588, just four years after the appearance of his original work, a pirated English-language version, *Mariners' Mirror*, appeared on the market. Such was its popularity that the word *waggoner* entered the English language as a synonym for pilots' guides.

The decorative nature of Waghenaer's charts is clearly illustrated in these examples showing the southwest coast of England and the coast of Portugal between Camino and Montegro. Note the water depth given in fathoms, the anchors denoting safe anchorages, and the inserted coastal profiles. In particular, the superior technique of engraving, the attractive strapwork cartouches, and the additional embellishment with the coat of arms, the compass rose, the ships, and the sea monsters make these desirable objects for any map collector.

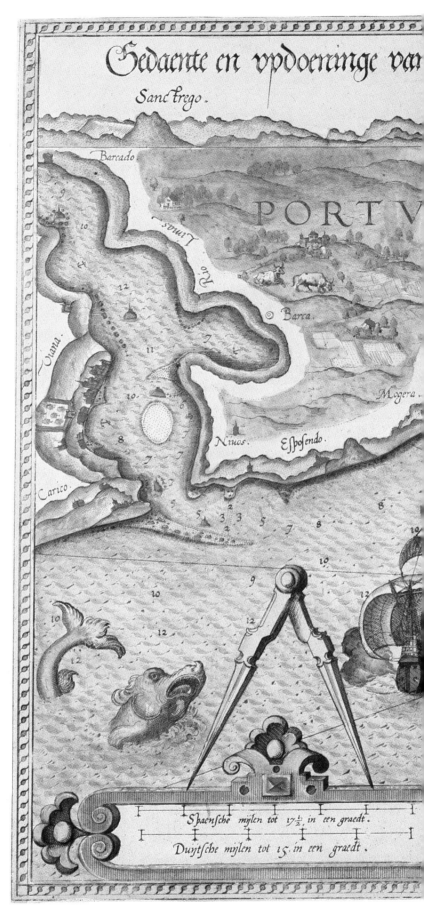

PLATE 31
Sea chart of the coast of
Portugal between Camino
and Montegro.
Lucas Jansz Waghenaer
(Enkhuizen, 1584).
12¹³⁄₁₆ x 20¹⁄₁₆", copper
engraving on paper.
From the pilot guide *The
Mariner's Mirror*.

Landt van Portugal, alst drie mijlen van v is, en daer beneffens zeijlt.

Als dit Swarte hoeuelken oost te zuijden van v leijt, soe ißmen open
voer die Riuier van Aueiro.

Montego.

GALLIÆ PARS

DIE WESTER ZEE

Cum Priuilegio
ad decennium.

Die Zee Caerte van Portugal, tußchen Camino en Montego, alsoe dat landt all daer in
sijn ghedaente is, met alle sijne haeuen enn
ondrepten, met groeter naersticheijt en vliedt
ghecorrigeert doer
Lucas Ianß Waghenaer vã Enchuijsen.
1583

PLATE 32
Sea chart of Europe.
Adriaen Gerritsen van
Haerlem (Amsterdam,
1591).
18½ x 23⅝", copper
engraving on vellum.

Paper is unsuitable for use aboard a ship. Most of the sea charts that have survived the centuries came from books and were never used at sea. Those actually used were thrown away after becoming obsolete, and few survived. Vellum, unlike paper, withstands the unfavorable conditions at sea rather well and so this material, despite its higher cost, was preferred by many. The manuscript portolano charts of the late Middle Ages were all drawn on vellum. In the late sixteenth and seventeenth centuries sea charts printed on vellum were issued in Amsterdam. One of these charts, depicted here, is the general chart of the European waters by the chart maker Adriaen Gerritsen of Haarlem. This chart has both latitude and longitude scales along its borders. The chart was issued by Cornelis Claesz, the leading publisher of sea charts and pilot books in Amsterdam, who also published Waghenaer's pilot guides.

Early in the fourteenth century Mediterranean mariners sailed as far as England and Flanders. It is likely that they wrote the first sailing directions of the western Euorpean waters, like the Mediterranean *portolanos*. Their colleagues must have appreciated these pilot guides and probably copied them, for parts of the oldest surviving hand-written sailing directions for western seas, the so-called *Seebuch*, are ascribed to the fourteenth century. These sailing directions were copied, corrected, and enlarged with the copier's own knowledge; in this way these hand-written sailing directions formed the material for the first printed rutters from the beginning of the sixteenth century. The oldest known printed pilot guides are Pierre Carcie's *La Routier de la Mer* and Robert Copland's *The Rutter of the Sea*, the latter being a translation from the former. Mediterranean mariners must have introduced the manuscript portolano or compass chart for western seas. The first printed sea charts appeared in the middle of the sixteenth century.

The first printed sea charts of the sixteenth century were, like nearly all maps of this era, woodcuts, a technique of printing in which the image is obtained by cutting away all parts of the surface of a block of wood that are to remain blank in the print. In this way the image is laid in relief on the surface of the block. To make a print, the parts in relief were inked and pressed upon a sheet of paper. The precision of reproduction was limited, just as was the number of prints that could be made from one block, for the lines soon wore away or broke off. For this reason relief printing of charts was soon to be superseded by intaglio printing, in which the lines to be printed were engraved in a plate of copper with the aid of the engraver's chisel. Ink was rubbed into these lines while the rest of the surface of the plate was kept clean. The plate, together with a sheet of slightly wetted paper, was pulled through a printing press; pressure caused the ink to be sucked into the paper, leaving an image on it. A copper engraving can always be recognized by the imprint of the plate around the print itself. This intaglio technique allowed for greater quality as well as quantity, for when the plate was worn down by the printing process, it could be refreshed by re-engraving the lines. In our eyes woodcut maps have a certain primitive charm lacking in the more refined copper engravings.

At the end of the sixteenth century printed rutters with woodcut charts between the text appeared on the market. These pilot guides soon became obsolete after the publication of Waghenaer's *Spieghel der Zeevaerdt* with its sophisticated engraved sea charts. Only a few of these rutters survived; one of them is *Die Caerte vande Oost en de West Zee* (*Charts of the East and West Sea*) by Goeyvaert Willemsen van Hollesloot, published in Harlingen (Holland) in 1588. Besides the written navigational instructions and sailing directions, it contains woodcuts of nautical instruments and woodcut charts of the coastal areas of southeast England, Holland, northeast Germany, and Norway.

The woodcut shown depicts the coastal area around Harlingen, on the north coast of the Netherlands.

PLATE 33
Sea chart of the Dutch coast near Harlingen.
Govaert Willemsen van Hollesloot (Harlingen, 1588).
9¹⁄₁₆ x 7¹⁄₁₆″, woodcut on paper.
From the pilot guide *Die Caerte vande Oost ende West Zee*.

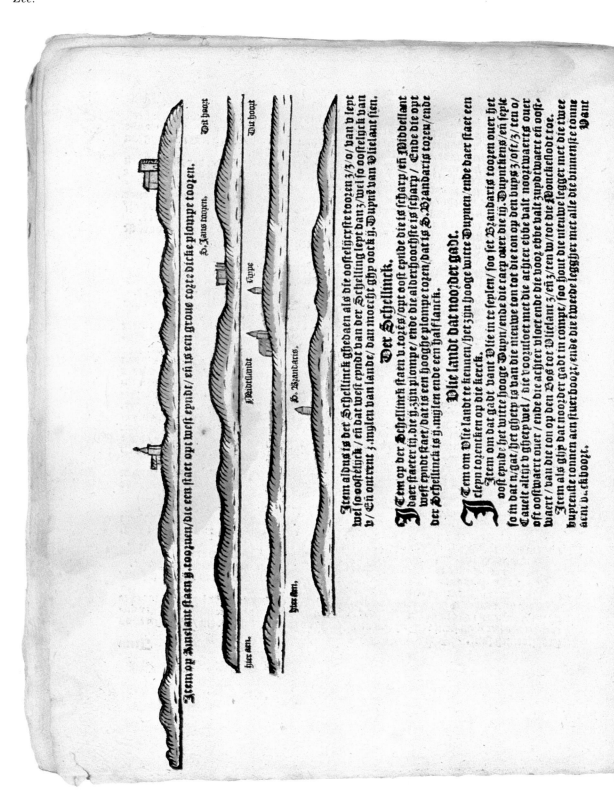

66

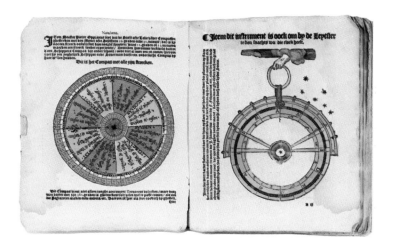

PLATE 34
Compass card, and
"nocturnal" instrument
which gives the observer the
hour of the night and the
position of the star Polaris.
From Govaert Willemsen
van Hollesloot's *Die Caerte
vande Oost ende West Zee*
(Harlingen, 1588).

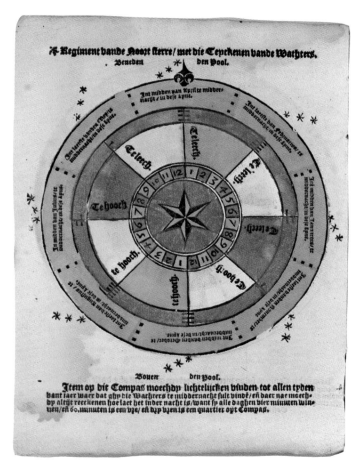

PLATE 35
Regiment of the North Star.
From Govaert Willemsen
van Hollesloot's *Die Caerte
vande Oost ende West Zee*
(Harlingen, 1588).

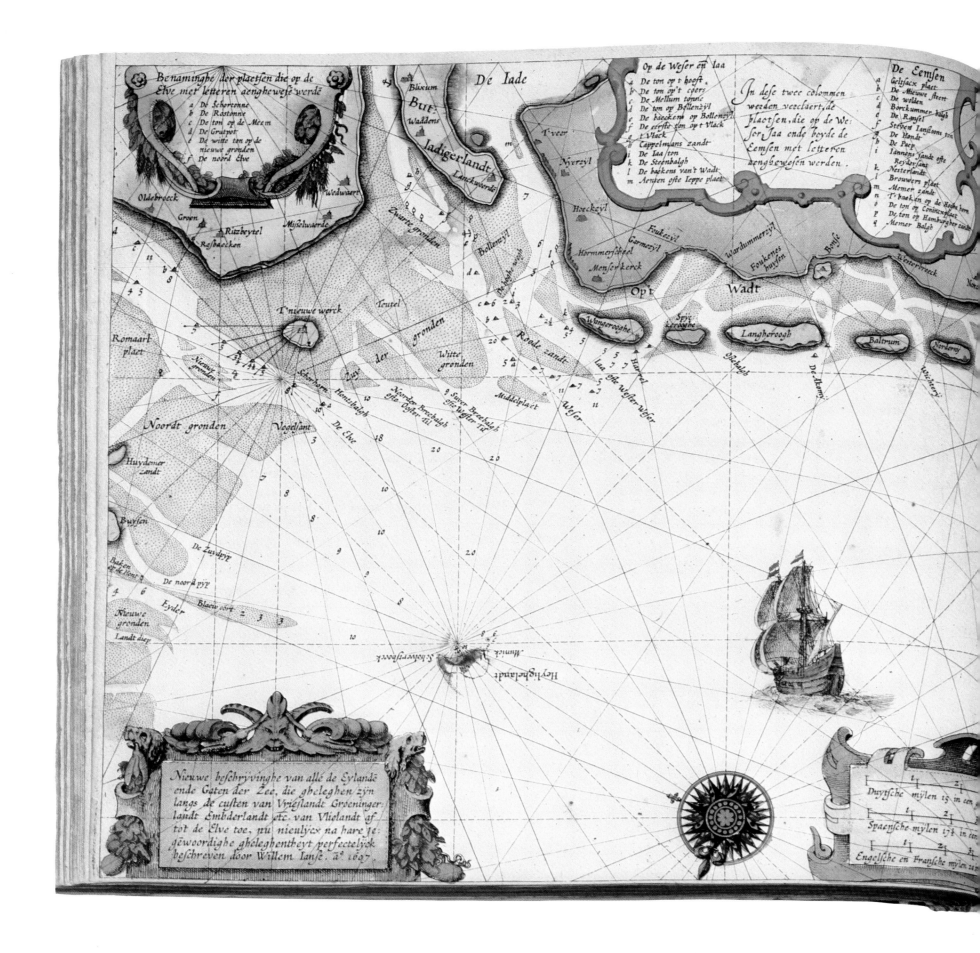

Willem Blaeu (1571–1638) was settled in Amsterdam in 1608 in the *die Guidne Sonnewizjer* ("the Guilded Sundial") when he published his first pilot book, *Het Licht der Zeevaart* (*The Light of Navigation*), containing an introduction to the art of northern, eastern, and western navigation.

It superseded Lucas Waghenaer's pilot books *De Spieghel der Zeevaerdt* and *De Thresoor der Zeevaerdt*, and adopted the small oblong folio form of Waghenaer's books.

In the introduction Willem Blaeu, pupil of the famous Danish astronomer Tycho Brahe, gave advice on the art of astronomical navigation,

such as the use of the nocturnal or night dial for finding time by means of the watchers of the polar star, the astrolabe, and the cross staff.

His charts were graduated for latitude in the margin, except for those of the Baltic and Arctic areas, due to the exaggerated errors of the plane chart close to the Pole. Blaeu also warned the mariner against the use of the plane chart for ocean voyages, referring to his chart of the West Indies based upon the Mercator projection. Blaeu's pilot book was an enormous success. It was translated into English (*The Light of Navigation*) and French (*Le Flambeau de la Naviga-*

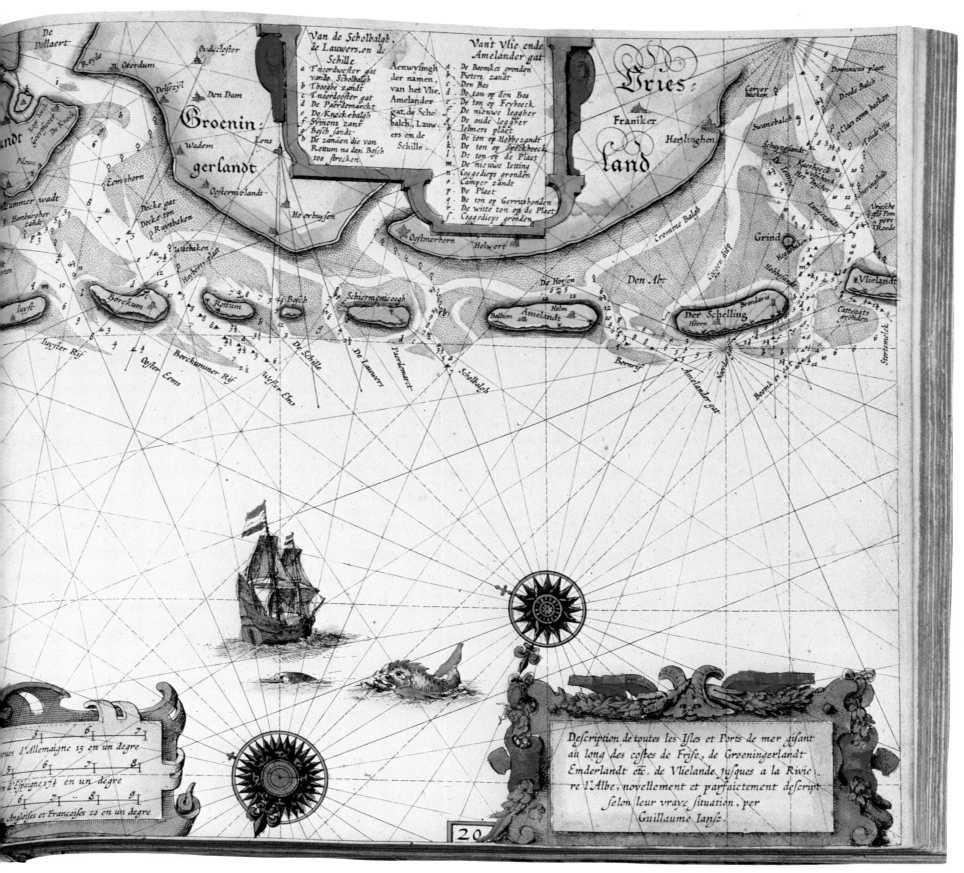

tion); it was published in twenty-four editions
between 1608 and 1646, including the pirated
editions of his rival, Johannes Janssonius. In
1618 it was enlarged with a third book covering
the navigation of the Mediterranean area. As
such it was the successor to Willem Barentsz's
Caertboeck van de Midlandtsche Zee. Challeng-
ing the ever-increasing competition of his neigh-
bor and rival, Johannes Janssonius, Willem
Blaeu published an enlarged pilot book, called *De
Zee-Spiegel (The Sea Mirror)* in 1623. It contained 111 charts, all completely reset and updated with the latest nautical information. Blaeu

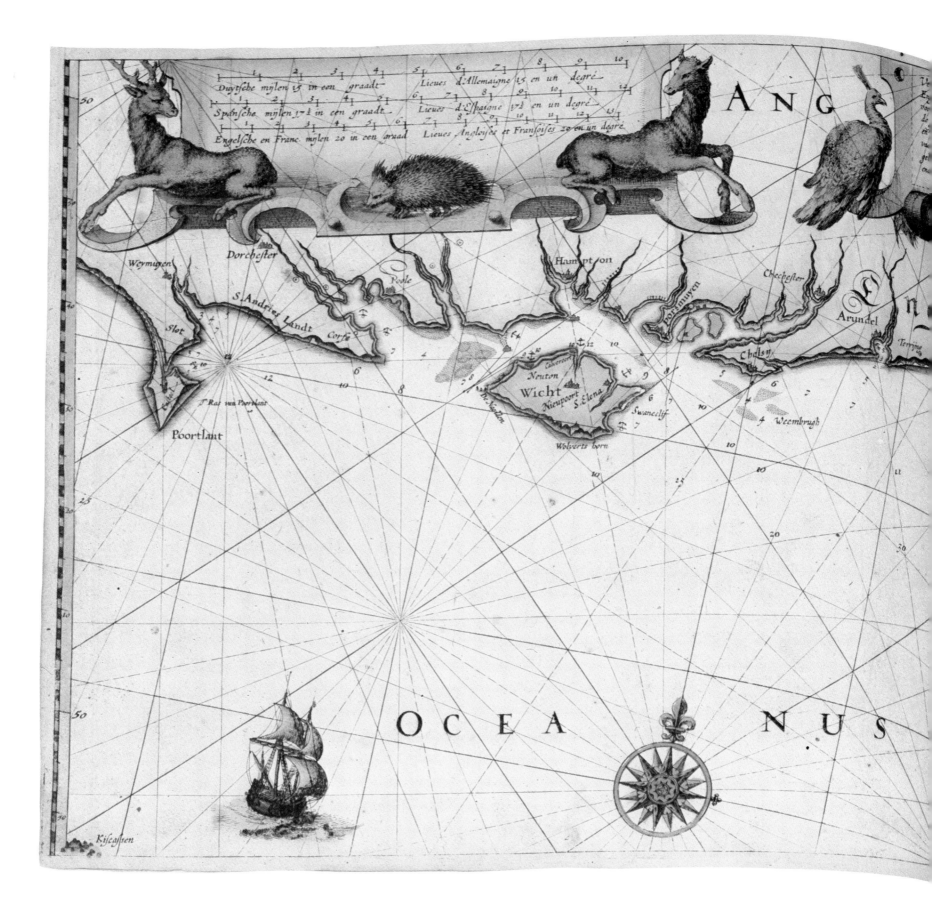

wrote in his introduction that he compiled and updated his charts with information he got from experienced mariners; they visited his shop near the water when they called at the port of Amsterdam.

There were eleven Dutch editions of the *Zee-Spiegel* between 1623 and 1658, two English editions (1625 and 1635) entitled *The Sea Mirror*, and two more English editions (1643 and 1653) called *The Sea Beacon*. After 1652 the name was changed to *De Groote Zee-Spiegel* (*The Great Sea Mirror*) and was in print until 1666.

In 1635 Willem Blaeu's abilities were officially recognized by his appointment as hydrographer to the Dutch East Indies Company. He held this important office until his death in 1638. He was succeeded by his son Johannes.

For decades mariners were directed by Blaeu's pilot books and they were used so much that few copies have survived. His market was seriously threatened, however, by the publication in 1632 of Jacob Colom's *Vyeriche Colomne*. Slowly Blaeu's prominent position in the field of hydrographical publications disappeared as the main interest of the firm shifted to other fields.

Willem Blaeu's charts depicted here show clearly the oblong-format of his pilot guide, a format preferred by the mariner of the first half of the seventeenth century over the folio-size of the chart in Lucas Janz Waghenaer's *Spieghel der Zeevaerdt*. Both charts are covered with lavishly decorated cartouches, compass roses, and animals.

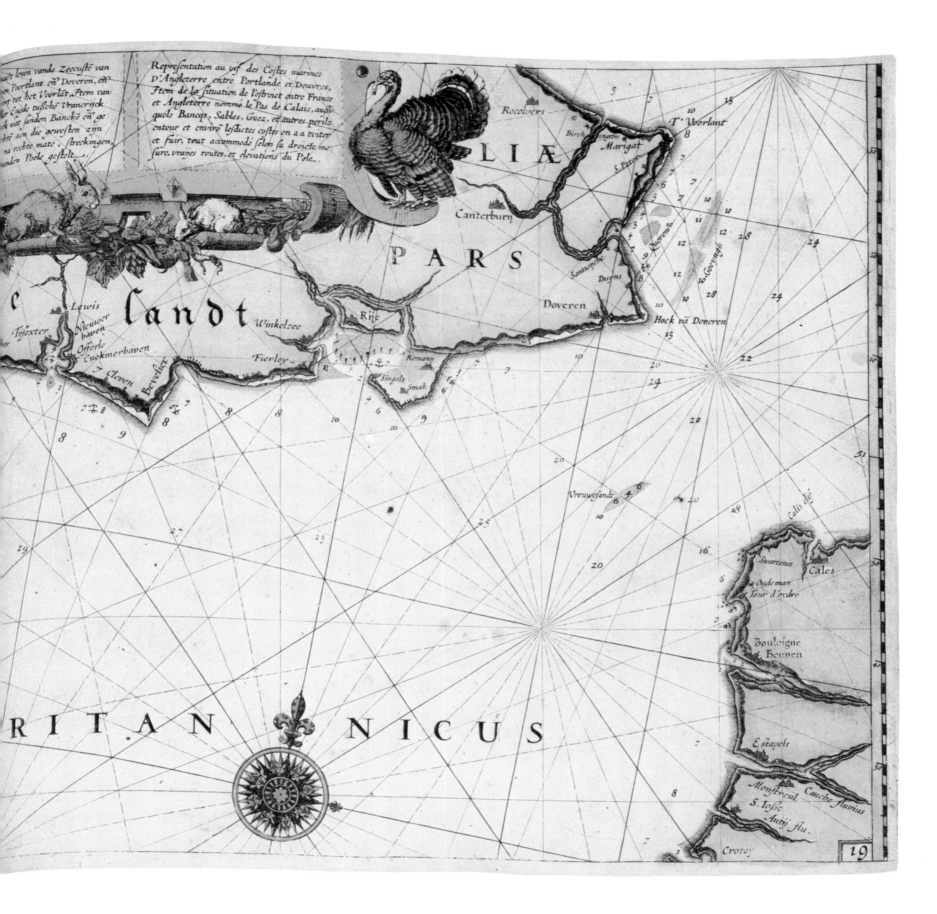

PLATE 37
Astronomical sextant.
Johannes Blaeu
(Amsterdam, 1663).
15¹⁵/₁₆ x 10⅝", copper
engraving on paper.
From the *Atlas Mayor*.

PLATE 38
Sea chart of the coast of
southeast England.
Willem Jansz Blaeu
(Amsterdam, 1608).
9⅝ x 21⅝", copper
engraving on paper.
From the pilot guide *The
Light of Navigation*.

In the age of the sail the elements played a much more prominent part than in motorized shipping today. Not only did the extreme conditions of the elements—hurricanes, tornadoes, and the like—take a heavy toll, but the difference between a favorable or an unfavorable wind or no wind at all meant the difference between life and death for the crew of the ships making their long voyages to the Asian seas. Life aboard was hard, the sanitary conditions were deplorable, and the conservation of food and water was a grave problem. Dysentery and scurvy caused many casualties, and the ship doctor's treatment often did more ill than good.

Favorable streams and winds shortened the voyage to a considerable degree, and the navigators to Asia were soon to learn the best times to depart and the routes to take. The compulsory sailing directions of the Dutch East Indies Company were based on knowledge gained the hard way. The outgoing fleet, headed for Java, left Europe in August, sailing south with the Canary Stream to a passage halfway into the southern Atlantic called the "cart path." On the African side was the area of the Guinea Stream, which went westwards, and of unfavorable winds; on the American side was the area of the equatorial streams that the Spaniards used on their way to the Lesser Antilles. It sometimes happened that a ship on its way to the East Indies drifted west of this passage and arrived in the West Indies instead. After passing this "cart path," the ships sought the Brazilian coast with its favorable Brazilian Stream and made for St. Helena off the West African coast for fresh food and water. For the crossing of the Indian Ocean the ships first sailed south until they reached the zone of the Westerlies and the South Australian Stream and held a course east until they were near the West Australian coast, then altered their course to northeast and headed toward Java.

The return fleet sailed in May from Batavia

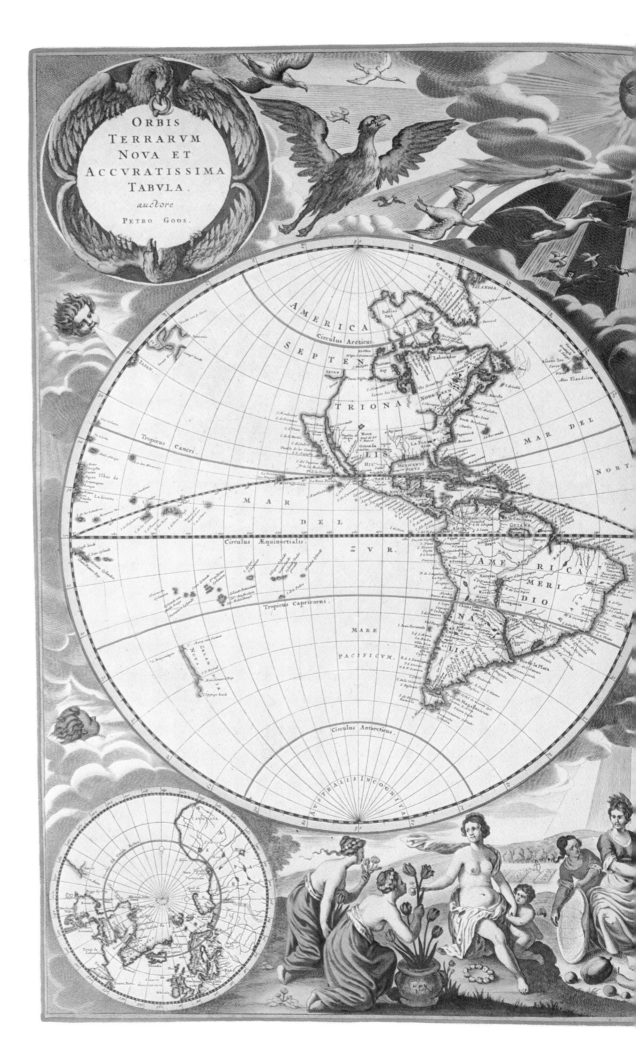

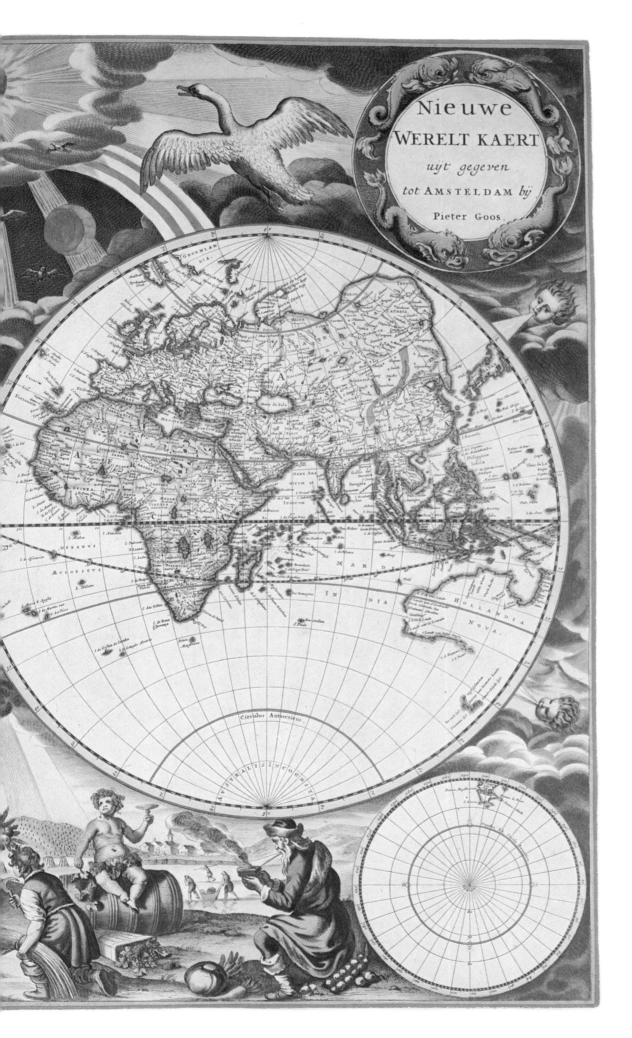

PLATE 39
Chart of the world.
Pieter Goos (Amsterdam,
1666).
17½ x 21½", copper
engraving on paper.
From the atlas *The Sea
Atlas of the Water World*.

(now Djakarta), steering the shortest route to Europe through the Indian Ocean and favored by the South Equatorial Stream and, after passing the Cape of Good Hope in the South Atlantic, by the Benguela Stream. After again passing the passage called the "cart path," they headed for Holland, which they reached via the Channel or, when the winds were unfavorable, by a route west of England between the Shetlands and the Faeroe Islands. After rounding the Cape of Good Hope between January and July, the Ceylon fleet turned north, sailing along the East African coast. Between July and January the ships sailed, like the Java fleet, eastwards in the zone of the western trade winds. They steered away from the coast of West Australia and turned instead to the north, sailing past the coasts of Java and Sumatra; then to reach Ceylon they changed course to the west when they had passed these islands.

The Spanish crossed the Pacific from America's west coast to the Philippines on a latitude of 16 degrees north, favored by the prevailing Easterlies. On their return voyage they sailed on 35 degrees north with the Japan Stream. For this reason they never discovered the Hawaiian Islands.

The decorative world chart of the Amsterdam publisher Pieter Goos from his sea atlas of 1666, *Orbis Terrarum Nova et Accuratissima Tabula*, shows the discoveries of the preceding years of the seventeenth century. The mythical Southland has disappeared, and the results of the two voyages made by the Dutchman Abel Tasman in the years 1642–43 and 1644 along Australia's and New Zealand's coasts are presented in the chart. In the Pacific the discoveries of the Spaniards Alvaro de Mendana, Pedro Fernandez de Quiros, and Luis Vaez de Torres and the Dutchmen Jacob Lemaire and Willem Schouten are shown. As usual in maps of this epoch, California is depicted as an island. In the two lower corners the polar areas are shown.

NORVEGIÆ MARITIMÆ
ab Elf-burgo ad Dronten

Pascaert van

NOORWEGEN

streckende van Elf-burg
tot Dronten.

Gedruckt by F. de Wit

GOUVERNEMENT van DRONTEN

GOUVERNEMENT van BERGEN

N O O R W E G

OCEANUS SEPTENTR

Frederick de Wit (1630–1706) had his shop in Amsterdam, named *In de Witte Paskaert* ("In the White Sea Chart"). In 1675 he published his sea atlas *Orbis Maritimus ofte Zee-atlas*. This atlas contained twenty-seven charts of the world as it was then known. These charts are embellished with finely etched cartouches. Comparing the cartouche in this chart by de Wit with, for instance, those in the charts of Lucas Waghenaer makes the difference clear. The cartouches of these late sixteenth-century charts have an ornamental character, adopted from architecture; the cartouches of the maps of the second half of the seventeenth century are often etched, a technique giving a looser impression. The image is not cut into the plate with the engraver's chisel, but is drawn with an etching needle in the etching ground, previously brought onto the plate. Then the plate is put into an acid bath. The ground protects the copperplate except in the lines opened with the needle. The acid bites the image into the plate. This technique does require the professional skill of the engraver.

After de Wit's death in 1706 the plates of these charts began a life of their own. They were used for almost a century, first by Louis Renard for his atlas *De la Navigation et du Commerce*, published in 1715 and 1739. After Renard, the plates were acquired by R. and J. Ottens and were used for an atlas published in 1745. Later the plates were obtained by the van Keulen publishing house.

Beginning in the fifteenth century the center of naval and mercantile power shifted from the eastern Mediterranean to Spain and Portugal. At the end of the sixteenth and the beginning of the seventeenth century the center again moved from these countries to the countries around the North Sea. Holland had its Golden Age during the seventeenth century but was too small to stay in the race during the eighteenth century. This left the French and English to fight for supremacy.

The history of marine cartography reflects these developments. The Italian republics of Venice, Genoa, and Florence were the first centers of hydrographical activities. The Italian portolano chart makers taught their trade to the Catalans and Majorcans. At the time of the Spanish and Portuguese discoveries and their subsequent hegemony during the sixteenth century, Seville and Lisbon were the centers of marine cartography. The School of Dieppe prospered in the middle of the sixteenth century and from there the center of publishing—now in printed form—moved via Antwerp to Amsterdam, where it remained during the seventeenth century. Without disparaging the achievements of hydrographers and publishers in other countries, one may say with only some exaggeration that the printed seventeenth-century sea chart was inevitably published in Amsterdam.

The greatest name in Dutch cartography is that of Blaeu: Willem Blaeu was the founder of the publishing house by that name, his son Johannes brought the firm to its highest achievement, never surpassed in the history of cartography: *The Atlas Mayor.*

This atlas, normally in twelve parts and up to then the largest book ever printed, could be enlarged according to the individual wishes of the patron. And to meet the most refined taste, its maps were colored and heightened with gold by accomplished artists and lavishly bound by master binders. It was one of the most esteemed gifts presented by the States General of the Dutch Republic.

Johannes Blaeu intended to enlarge *The Atlas Mayor* with a sea atlas, but he did not live to realize this plan. For this reason the Goos sea atlas is often bound together with the other volumes of *The Atlas Mayor.*

The chart of Europe is from this magnificent atlas and is probably colored by the master colorist Dirck van Santen (1637/38–1708). With only a few exceptions the colorists worked in obscurity; van Santen is one of these exceptions. He is mentioned by his contemporaries as an especially gifted colorist. The chart is embellished with coats-of-arm of the reigning monarchs of Europe. The inland parts of Africa are used to depict the eastern part of the Mediterranean.

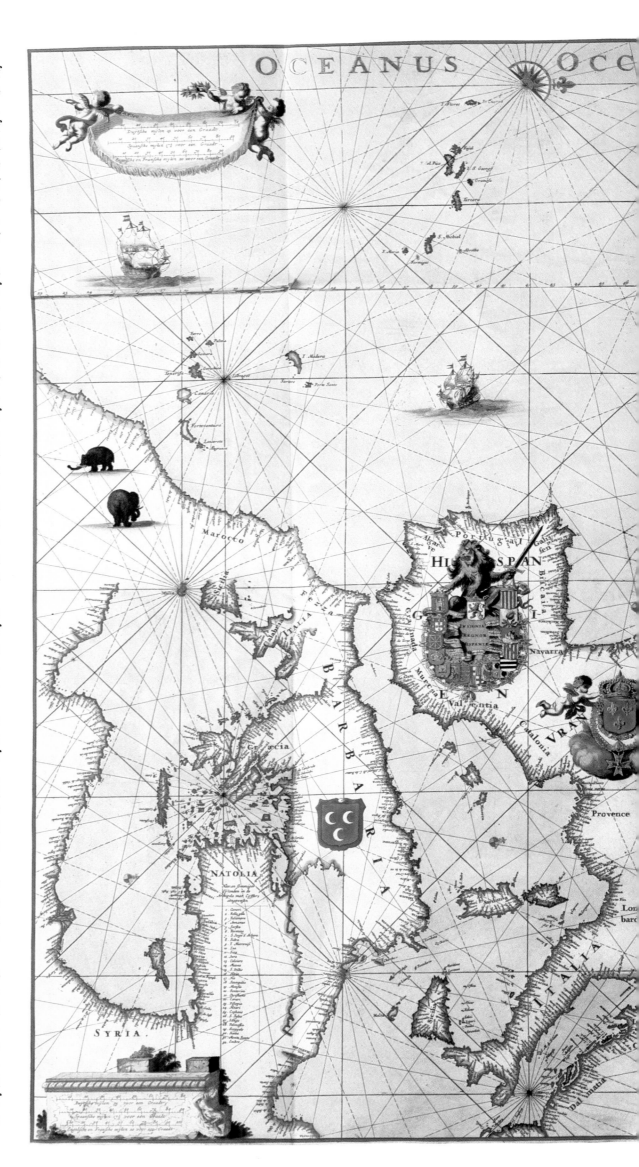

PLATE 41
Sea chart of the coasts of Europe.
Willem Jansz Blaeu and Johannes and Pieter Blaeu (Amsterdam, 1677).
$30^{11}/_{16}$ x $38^{5}/_{8}$", copper engraving on paper.

Johannes van Keulen (1654–1715) was the founder of the famous publishing house of sea atlases and pilot guides that existed from 1678 until 1885. The most important works of the van Keulens are the sea atlas *Zee-atlas ofte Water-werelt* and the pilot guide *de Zeefakkel*.

Johannes van Keulen was not a cartographer himself so he secured the cooperation of the mathematician Claes Vooght, who prepared most of the charts published by Johannes van Keulen. Between 1679 and 1683 Johannes van Keulen and Claes Vooght produced the pilot guide *de Zeefakkel* in five parts, containing in the first edition 116 charts. The number of charts grew steadily in the following editions.

The *Zeefakkel* was the first printed pilot guide with charts covering all navigated waters of the world—only the charts of the East Indian Archipelago were kept secret by the Dutch East Indies Company.

The *Zee-atlas* was published between 1680 and 1734, growing from 40 charts in the first edition to 185 charts in the atlas edited by Johannes's son Gerard van Keulen in 1710. The charts were used both in the sea atlas and in the pilot guide.

The success of both atlas and pilot guide was enormous and when Hendrik Doncker died in 1699, Johannes van Keulen bought his stock, becoming the most important publisher of charts in Amsterdam. His competitors, Robijn and de Wit, had to be content with only a small part of the market.

The chart depicts Holland and the former Zuiderzee, now closed by a dike. The city of Amsterdam is situated on the border of the Zuiderzee.

After the fall of Antwerp in 1585 and the subsequent closing by the Dutch of its waterway to the sea, the river Scheldt, the city declined rapidly and its position in the European maritime trade was taken over by Amsterdam. The Netherlands was favorably situated between southwest Europe and the countries of the North Sea and the Baltic. Because large-scale demand and supply of cargo made regular sailings to all parts of Europe possible and a well-organized system of naval insurance and low rates of interest feasible, the Dutch Republic prospered. Holland had its Golden Age and Amsterdam was its center.

For a long time the Dutch mercantile fleet was larger than the combined fleets of England, Scotland, and France, and Amsterdam handled two-fifths of Dutch shipping, making it the largest port in the world.

PLATE 42
Plan and view of the city
of Amsterdam.
Gerard van Keulen and
Jacob De La Feuille
(Amsterdam, 1734).
20¹¹⁄₁₆ x 39³⁄₁₆″, copper
engraving on paper.
From the pilot guide *De
Nieuwe Groote Ligtende
Zeefakkel.*

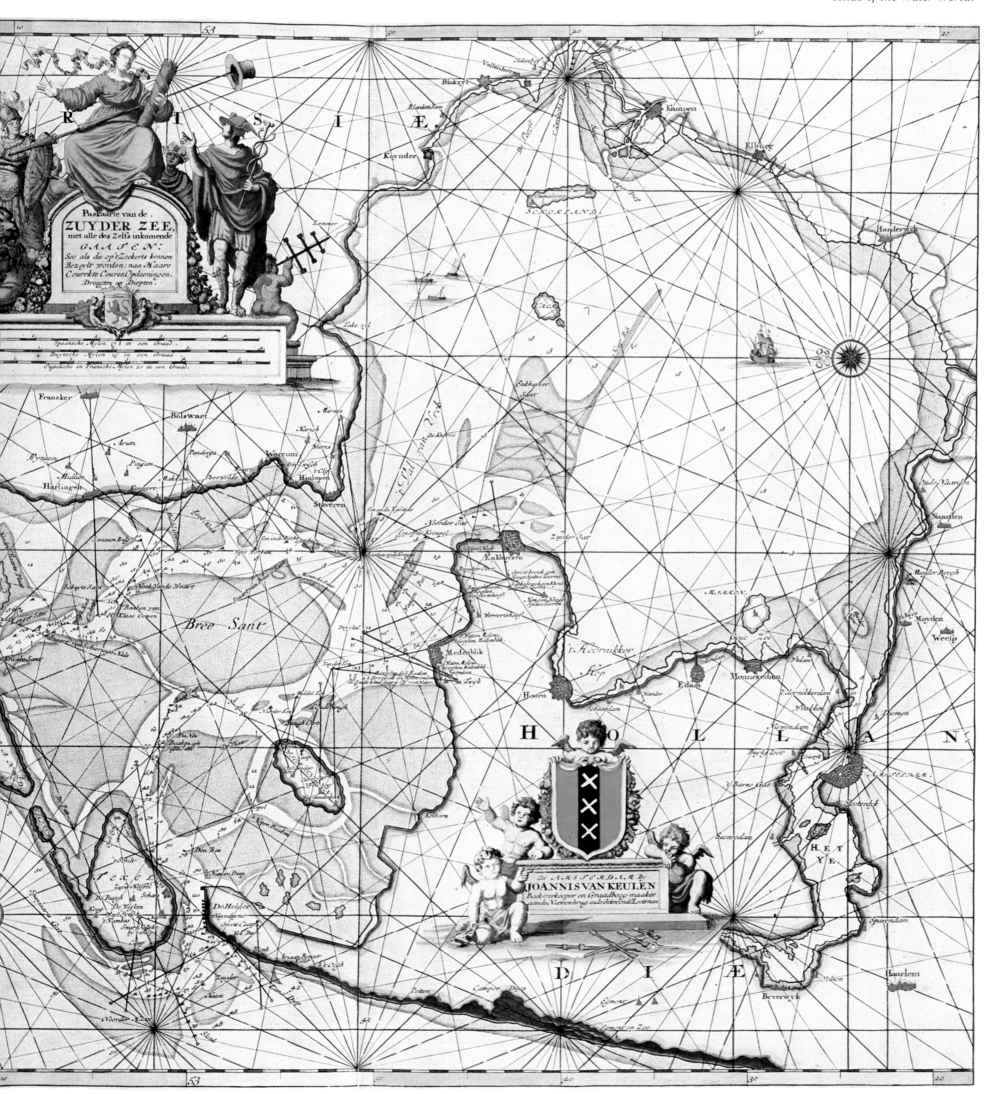

PLATE 43
Sea chart of the Zuiderzee,
Holland.
Johannes van Keulen
(Amsterdam, c. 1680).
20¹/₁₆ x 22⁷/₁₆″, copper
engraving on paper.
From the atlas *The Sea
Atlas of the Water World*.

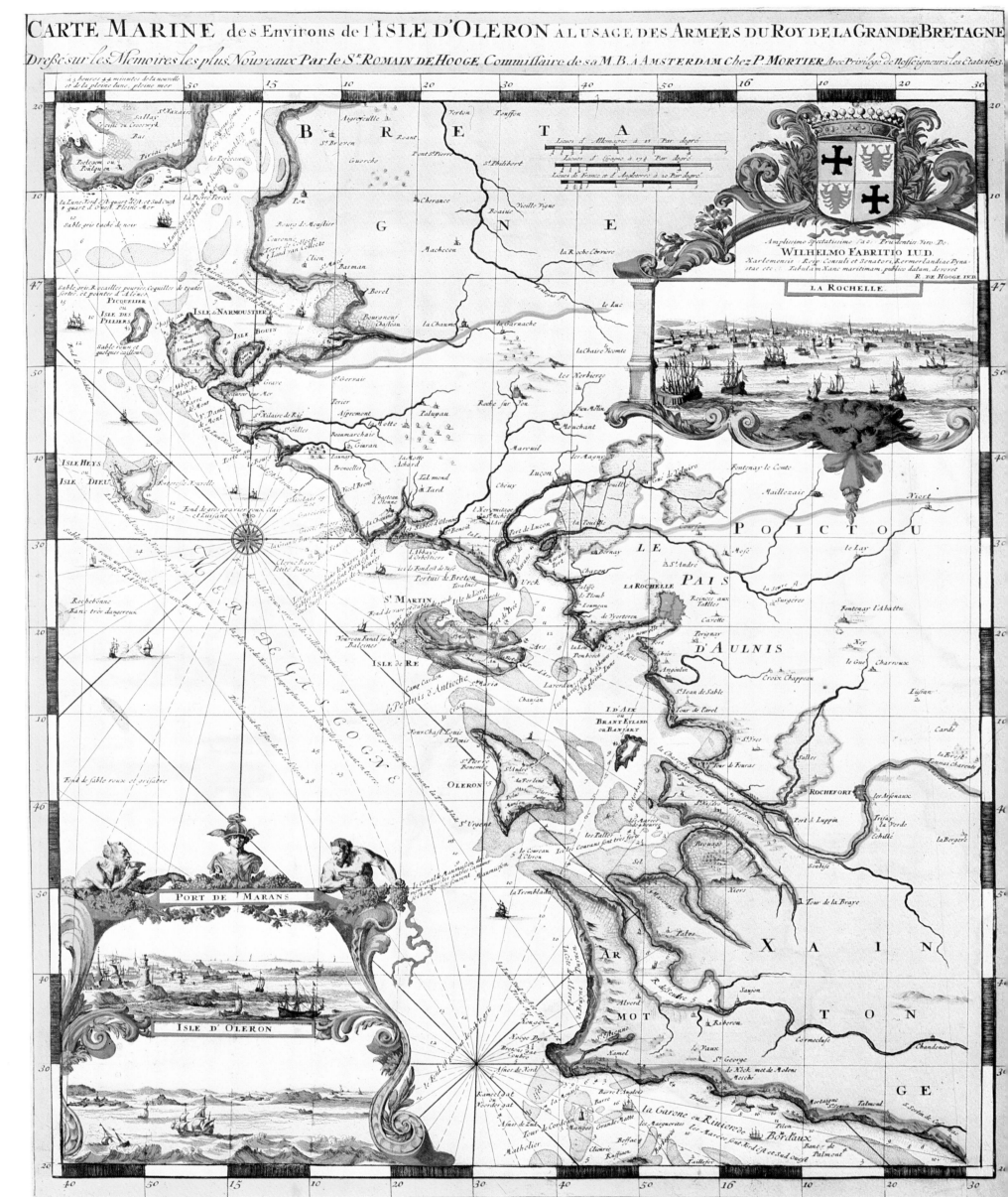

CARTE MARINE des Environs de l'ISLE D'OLERON AL USAGE DES ARMÉES DU ROY DE LA GRANDE BRETAGNE

Dressé sur les Memoires les plus Nouveaux Par le Sr ROMAIN DE HOOGE, Commissaire de sa M.B. à AMSTERDAM chez P. MORTIER Avec Privilege de Nosseigneurs les Etats 1693.

WILHELMO FABRITIO IUD.

LA ROCHELLE

PORT DE MARANS

ISLE D'OLERON

80

HOLLANDSE ADMIRAAL   FRANSE ADMIRAAL

The wealthy and successful publisher Pieter Mortier was the scion of a French Huguenot family. Through his French connections, he contributed to the development of cartography by publishing the work of French cartographers such as Sanson. In 1693, together with the Paris publisher Jules Jaillot, he published the presumptuous sea atlas *Neptune François*, which had twenty-nine charts of exceptionally large format ($22^{13}/_{16}$ x $37^{3}/_{8}''$) showing the coastal waters of Europe (except for those of the Mediterranean). The charts were done by French cartographers such as Pené and Cassini, and although the volume was engraved and printed in Amsterdam, it can be considered the first printed French sea atlas.

Another atlas, frequently bound together with the *Neptune François*, was the *Atlas Maritime: Carte Marine à l'usage du Roy de la Grande Bretagne (Sea Charts to Be Used by the King of Great Britain)*. Composed of only nine charts of the European coastal waters from Holland southward, it included one unusually large (23 x $54^{3}/_{4}''$) chart of the Mediterranean. This magnificent atlas was commissioned by William III of Orange during his dual reign as stadholder of the United Provinces of the Northern Netherlands and king of England—a title he held by virtue of his marriage to Mary, sister of the previous king of England.

Better suited to the taste of kings than to actual use at sea, this atlas, based on English manuscript charts, was hand-drawn by the famous Dutch book illustrator Romeijn de Hooghe. The nine charts are abundantly embellished with

cartouches and insets of harbors of the areas depicted. Hand-colored and gold-heightened by accomplished artists, these charts are each in their own right highlights in the history of cartography.

In 1700 Pieter Mortier issued a third volume, *Suite de Neptune François*, with thirty-seven charts of the non-European harbors. These charts were not updated, as was the usual custom with sea charts, nor were they republished, except for the first volume, which was reissued in 1703. These facts prove that the atlas was used in libraries and not at sea. The title *Neptune François* also began a life of its own since it was subsequently used for several eighteenth-century French hydrographical works such as Bellin's *Sea-Atlas* of 1753.

This chart of the French coast in the vicinity of the island of Orleron is one of nine that comprised the *Atlas Maritime* by Romeijn de Hooghe and Pieter Mortier. This collection depicted the stages of the naval engagements between the French and the English and their respective allies between 1684 and 1815, in the coastal waters of the English Channel, the Atlantic, and the Mediterranean.

During this period, the fleets of the two nations were fighting each other for supremacy in the overseas trade and the colonies abroad. The English tried blockading the French coast to make French trade impossible and so, in an indirect way, to starve that country's possessions abroad. The French, in turn, aimed at breaking the blockade and invading England.

The relations between the Amsterdam publishers of sea charts in the second half of the seventeenth century are rather confusing. Despite his name, there is no relation between Johannes Loots, or Lootsman, and the Lootsman family. Johannes Loots started his career as a nautical instrument maker, afterward turning to publishing sea charts. In 1675 he had a shop near the waterfront of Amsterdam named *Inde jonge Lootsman*, where he published his sea atlas *Het nieu en compleet Paskaart Boek van de Noord en de Oost Zee* in 1697. The plates for this atlas were engraved by Antonie de Winter. Together with de Winter and the mathematician Claes de Vries, he published several charts with increasing latitudes.

The chart depicted is from the atlas mentioned above. All ships passing the Sound—the water that separates Denmark from Sweden and the entrance to the Baltic—had to pay a toll, thus quantitative data about shipping to and from the Baltic still exist. From these data it appears that of the total number of ships passing the Sound in the entire seventeenth century, Dutch shipping averaged around sixty percent. The most important ports of commerce were Danzig (Gdansk) and Königsberg (now Kaliningrad). In these ports the ships were loaded with timber and corn after they had unloaded their cargo of dairy products, herring, salt, and luxurious Eastern products like wine, silk, and spices.

Freedom of trade was of interest to the Dutch and their maritime actions in the Sound were always aimed at that goal.

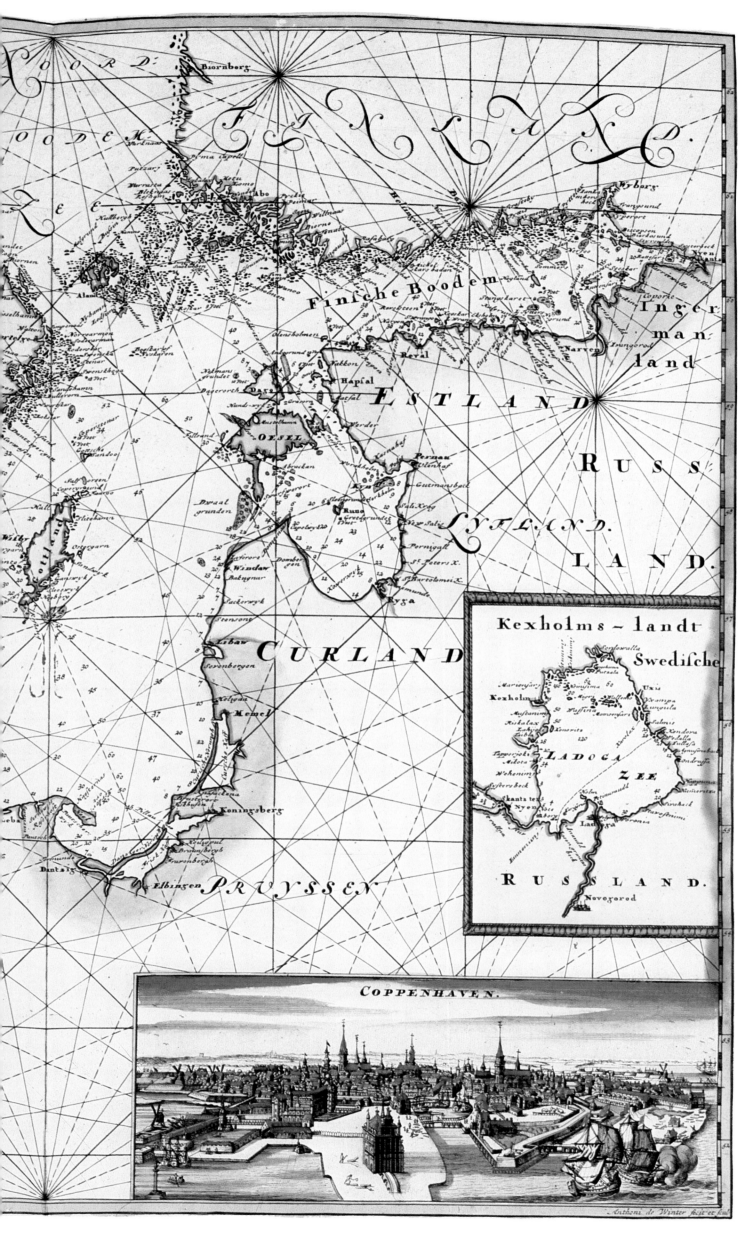

PLATE 45
Sea chart of the Baltic.
Johannes Loots
(Amsterdam, 1697).
20¼ x 22¹³⁄₁₆″, copper
engraving on paper.
From the atlas *The New and
Complete Sea Chart Book of
the North Sea and the Baltic.*

83

NORTH ATLANTIC

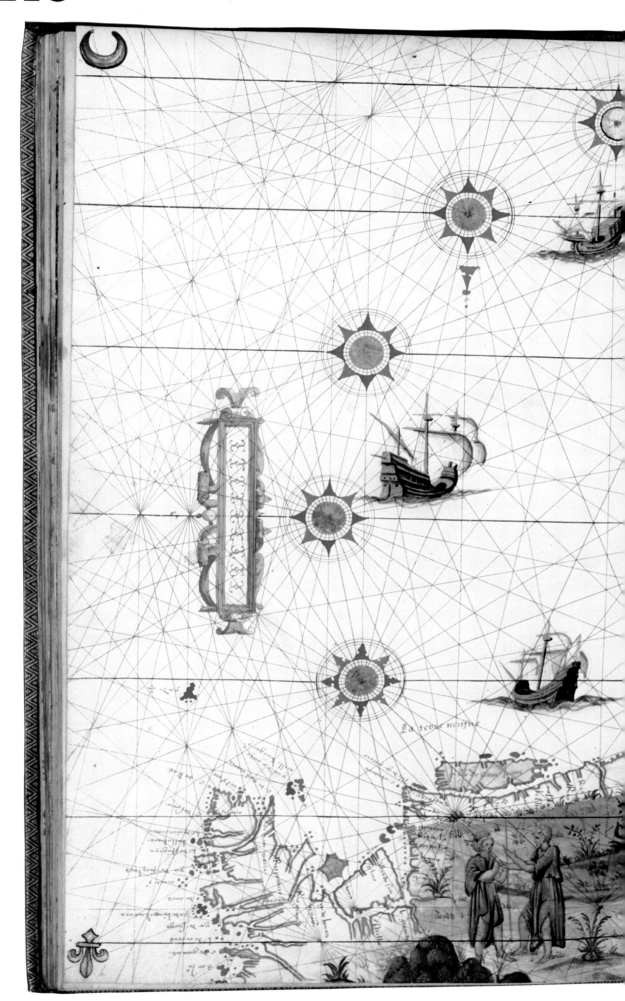

Irish monks were perhaps the first Europeans to set eyes on the American continent. The chronicle of the voyages of St. Brendan tells of his explorations of a "Land of Promise." There is evidence that this was America's mainland.

More is known about the voyages of the Norsemen in the tenth century. Icelandic sagas tell of the attempted colonization of the lands southwest of Greenland. Norsemen sailed southward from Greenland, and from their accounts it appears that they reached New England, which they named Vineland for the wild grapes they found there.

This information was not completely lost in the following centuries, but to the southern European scholar of the fifteenth century, it was a mere rumor from a distant corner of the world.

In the fifty years after Columbus's first landfall, the northeast coast of America was explored in search of a northern passage to China. The Venetian Giovanni Caboto, or John Cabot as the English called him, was the first to reach North America. In 1497 he sailed from Bristol with a patent of discovery by the English king Henry VII. He reached the coast below 56 degrees north latitude and sailed south to the present-day Carolinas. In 1517 his son Sebastian reached as far north on the American coast as 67.5 degrees north. He probably entered Hudson Bay and surveyed the coast almost as far south as Florida.

In 1499 Joao Fernandes, a *laborador*, or small landowner, sailed from Lisbon in the service of King Manuel and reached the land that he named Labrador. In 1500 Gaspar Corte-Real, also searching for the supposed route to China, discovered Newfoundland. The Portuguese, convinced by these vain attempts that there was no such route, ceased their explorations in these regions. Their fishing fleets, however, kept visiting the rich fishing grounds off the coast of Newfoundland until quite recently. In 1524 Giovanni Verrazano, a Florentine in the service of the French king Francis I, explored the coastline from South Carolina to Newfoundland. He sailed along the Outer Bank Islands which separate Pamlico Sound from the Atlantic Ocean. He mistook them for an isthmus and the sound for the Pacific Ocean. Although he missed Chesapeake

Bay, he was probably the first European to enter New York Bay and the Hudson River. Verrazano met a terrible death; in 1528 he was killed and eaten by Caribbean natives before the eyes of his helpless brother and crew.

In 1534 the Frenchman Jacques Cartier entered the Gulf of St. Lawrence by way of the Strait of Belle Isle and circled the gulf. How-

84

PLATE 46
Portolano of the east coast
of North America.
Anonymous, School of
Dieppe (Dieppe, c. 1538).
16½ x 24¹³/₁₆″, manuscript
on vellum.
From an untitled atlas.

ever, he missed the mouth of the St. Lawrence River and Cabot Strait, between Nova Scotia and Newfoundland.

The chart shown is taken from an anonymous French atlas, dating from about 1540. It is one of the earliest representations of the northeastern coast of America, but Cartier's discoveries of 1534–35 are not depicted. The geographical material of the atlas is probably by a Portuguese chart maker working in Dieppe. If so, that would prove that a link existed between Portuguese cartographers and the School of Dieppe. The decorative elements in the borders and the land areas are by a French artist; the map shows no knowledge of the indigenous animals and plants of North America.

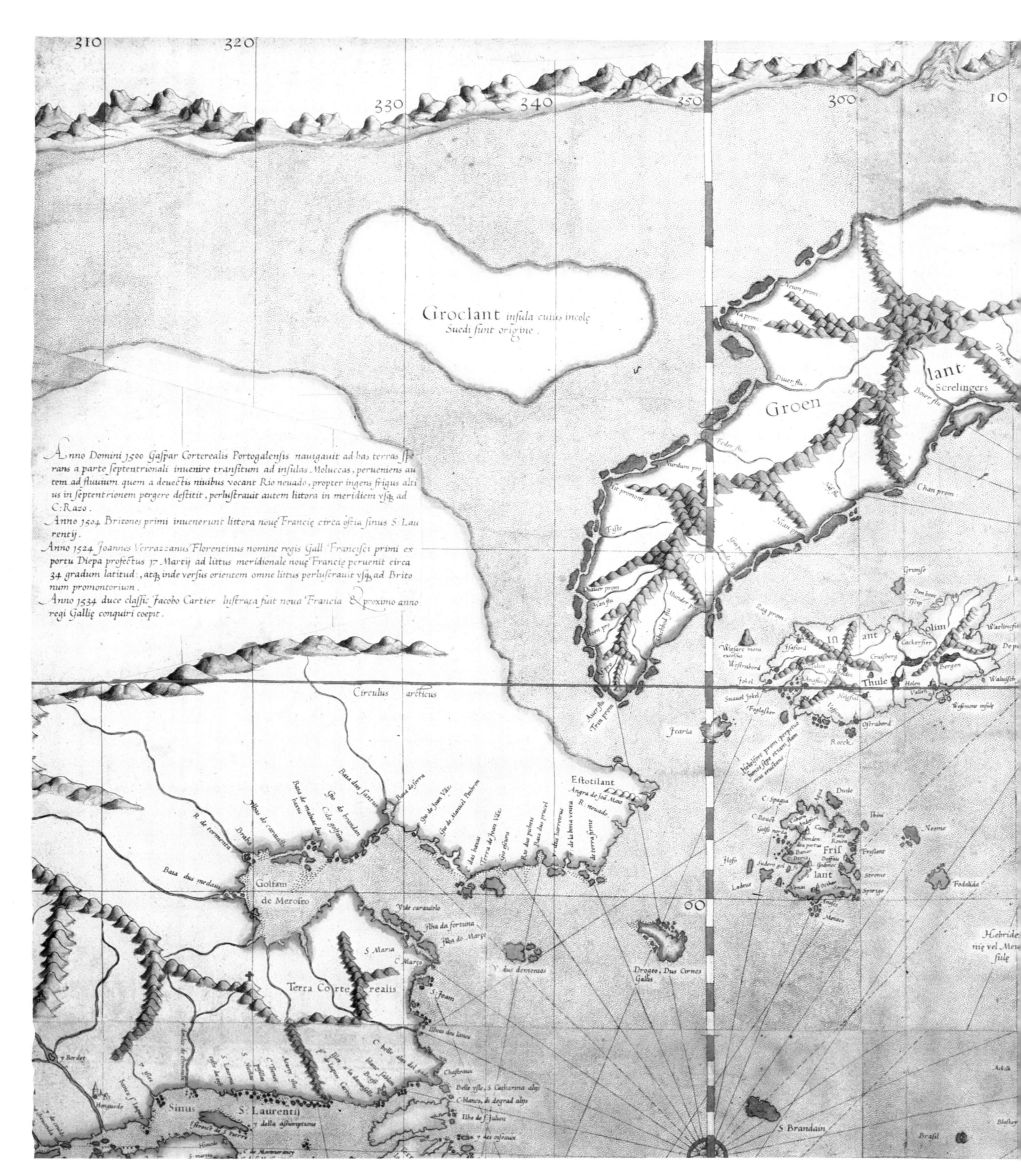

330   340   250   300   10

Groclant *insula cuius incolę Suedi sunt origine.*

Nærum prom.

Sich. prom.

Groen lant Srelingers

Diuer. flu.

Feder. flu.

Virdum prom.

Hit promont.

Næf. flu.

Chan. prom.

Fisfe

Afian flu.

70

Danær. prom.

Hanflu.

Steen pro.

Murder F.

Grunse La

Den houc

Tfiep

Reig prom.

Wdsfare mons excelsus

In ant

Olim Cackersier Warlincfion

Depe

Sige

Witsare mons excelsus
Westraborde

Hafiord

Cruisberg

Bergen

Walwsich

Aucr. flu. Trou prom.

Jokel

Thule Holm Vallen

Snauel Jokel

Fogliasser

Nelgfiord

Wesimone insule

Anno Domini 1500 Gaspar Corterealis Portogalensis nauigauit ad has terras speran: a parte septentrionali inuenire transitum ad insulas. Moluccas, perueniens autem ad fluuium quem a deuectis niuibus vocant Rio neuado, propter ingens frigus altius in septentrionem pergere destitit, perlustrauit autem littora in meridiem vsq, ad C: Razo.

Anno 1504 Britones primi inuenerunt littora nouę Francię circa ostia sinus S: Laurentij.

Anno 1524 Joannes Verrazzanus Florentinus nomine regis Gall: Francisci primi ex portu Diepa profectus 17 Martij ad littus meridionale nouę Francię peruenit circa 34 gradum latitud:, atq, inde versus orientem omne littus perlustrauit vsq, ad Britonum promontorium.

Anno 1534 duce classi: Jacobo Cartier lustrata fuit noua Francia & proximo anno regi Gallię conquiri coepit.

Jcaria

Roeck

Ofraborde

Circulus arcticus

C. Spagna

Dudo

Bona de iad. Maio Estotilant
Angra de iod: Maio

R: neuado

C: Bouet

Ihon

Neome

Goffo

Frisi
lant Friflant

Buta dus fantru:
Buta lafura
Ora de brandan

Gho. de maabuc. Iha:

Gho: de Juan Vĕı:

Co:lo stefana

Gho de Manuel Paucboren

R de tormenta

Hofo

Iederco

Stremoe

Draffa

Terra de Juan Vĕı.

Ade baxas
Gho ofiana

Rio dus pisseres

Buta dus praet.

de la bona vitca

Fodhda

Monaco

Bata dus medaus

Golfam de Merofro

Y de carauclo

Alha da fortuna

Y dus demonas

Drogto, Dus Cornes Gallis

Hebride nię vel Meu: siulę

Iha do Março

S: Maria C: Março

Terra Corte realis

S: Foam

Illons dus lariex

Chastcaux

Belle ysle, S: Catharina altą
C: Blanco, ib degrad altą

S: Brandain

Brasil

Blasker

Addi

Sinus S: Laurentij

y della assumptione

PLATE 47
Sea chart of the North Atlantic.
Gerard Mercator
(Duisburg, 1569).
17⁵⁄₁₆ x 24³⁄₁₆", copper engraving on paper.
Part of Mercator's world chart.

The part of the Mercator world chart, depicted here in eighteen sheets, shows the northern part of the Atlantic, the northernmost parts of Europe, America, Greenland, and part of the polar area. This chart is interesting because it disseminated a number of cartographical mistakes in the depiction of the area northwest of Ireland. The source of these mistakes is the imagined itinerary of a voyage supposedly made by the Venetian brothers Nicolo and Antonio Zeno at the end of the fourteenth century.

Shortly before Mercator had finished his chart, this work together with a map of this area, dated 1380, was published in Venice. On the basis of this evidence, the Venetians claimed the first discovery of the mainland of America. Unfortunately Mercator believed the story and offered the "Zenomap" as his authority. Mercator incorporated its information into this part of his chart. Thus appeared the nonexistent island of Friesland, south of Thule (Iceland), just like the islands of Brazil, and S. Brandain, referring to the Irish monk who sailed the waters west of Ireland. For the first time the name Estoti-land appears on the coast of America.

87

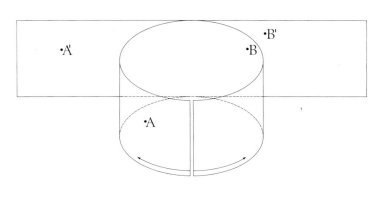

Gerard Mercator (1512–1594) is considered by many to have been the most important cartographer since Ptolemy. Nearly all modern sea charts are constructed by the method he first employed in his nautical world chart of 1569.

Born near Antwerp, he was the pupil of the mathematician Gemma Frisius. His first known map is dated 1537. In 1552 he moved to Duisburg, Germany, where he worked until his death on the *Atlas*, his major work, published between 1585 and 1594. With the publication of his chart of 1569, Mercator solved the problem that mariners had struggled with since the Portuguese began sailing the Atlantic: the development of a chart suitable for navigating great distances.

Such a chart has to accurately represent the earth's surface. That presents the problem of depicting the curvature of the globe on a flat plane.

The medieval chart maker thought the earth was flat. The resulting discrepancy in his maps was negligible for short-distance coastal navigation, but considerable and dangerous for long distance ocean travel.

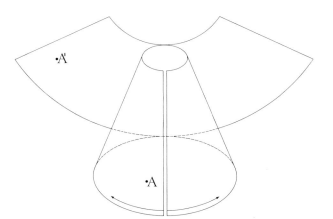

The scale of a chart reflects the reduction of real distances necessary for representation. Reducing the scale of a map increases the portion of the earth's surface it shows.

A globe's surface can never be unfolded on a plane, but the surfaces of a cylinder and a cone can be; when they are unwrapped they yield a rectangle and a segment of a circle, respectively.

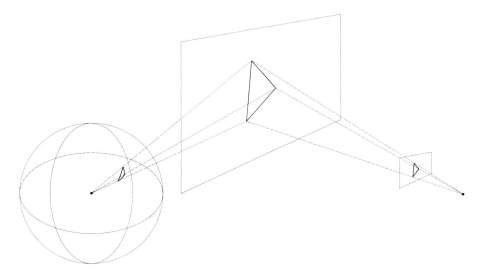

Mercator's chart depicted the earth's true form by projecting its globular surface onto a plane. Radiating from the earth's center are lines that cut the surface of the earth and form an image of it on an imaginary plane; next, this image is reduced until it can be accommodated on the chart itself.

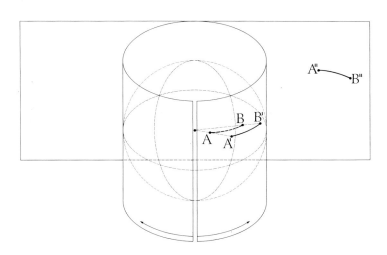

Thus the earth is "pumped up" until it presses against the inside of an imaginary cylinder or cone. This cylinder or cone is then unwrapped into either a rectangle or a segment of a circle.

Projection charts approximate reality, yet always with some distortion, particularly in the representation of the polar areas. Projection

charts are based upon the concepts of geographical latitude and longitude. Any position on the earth's surface can be defined by these coordinates. This is also true of its representation on a chart. When the latitude and longitude of a position are known, the position can be plotted using the latitude and longitude lines on the chart.

To be used aboard a ship, a chart must meet several requirements. First it must be able to represent a ship's course as a straight line. The second requirement is that of conformity, meaning that the angles between the course line and the latitude and longitude lines on the chart must be equal to the angles between the desired course and the latitude and longitude circles on earth.

Derived from the medieval "compass charts," the plane chart has meridians and parallels drawn in such a way that together they form a grid of squares. The distance between any two meridians is constant and equals the distance between any two parallels.

In reality, however, meridians, going from the equator to either pole, converge and meet at each pole. This means that the plane chart does not come up to the requirement of conformity. It cannot be used when great distances are covered.

This problem is elegantly solved by Mercator's projection method. Going toward the poles, the distance between the meridians measured along the parallels is reduced according to a mathematical function called the cosine. In order to meet the requirements of parallel meridians, however, it is necessary to keep a constant distance between the meridian on the chart, which will then also fulfill the requirement of conformity. To do this, one must increase the distance between the parallels on the chart by reversing the function by which the distance between meridian circles decreases in the direction of the poles. Mercator first applied this solution in his nautical world chart in 1569. A legend in this chart reads:

To the readers of this chart, greeting.
In making this representation of the world we had three preoccupations: Firstly, to spread on a plane the surface of the sphere in such a way that the positions of places shall correspond on all sides with each other both in so far as true direction and distance are concerned and as concerns correct longitudes and latitudes; then, that the forms of the parts be retained, so far as is possible, such as they appear on the sphere. With this intention we have had to employ a new proportion and a new arrangement of the meridians with reference to the parallels. Indeed, the forms of the meridians, as used till now by geographers, on account of their curvature and their convergence to each other, are not utilisable for navigation; besides, at the extremities, they distort the forms and positions of regions so much, on account of the oblique incidence of the meridians to the parallels, that these cannot be recognised nor can the relation of distances be maintained. On the charts of navigators the degrees of longitude, as the various parallels are crossed successively towards the pole, become gradually greater with reference to their length on the sphere, for they are throughout equal to the degrees on the equator, whereas the degrees of latitude increase not at all, so that, on these charts also, the shapes of regions are necessarily very seriously stretched and either the longitudes and latitudes or the directions and distances are incorrect; thereby great errors are introduced of which the principal is the following: if three places forming any triangle on the same side of the equator be entered on the chart and if the central one, for example, be correctly placed with reference to the outer ones as to accurate directions and distances, it is impossible that the outer ones be so with reference to each other. It is for these reasons that we have progressively increased the degrees of latitude towards each pole in proportion to the lengthening of the parallels with reference to the equator; thanks to this device we have obtained that, however two, three or even more than three, places be inserted, provided that of these four quantities: difference of longitude, difference of latitude, distance and direction, any two be observed for each place associated with another, all will be correct in the association of any one place with any other place whatsoever and no trace will anywhere be found of any of those errors which must necessarily be encountered on the ordinary charts of shipmasters, errors of all sorts, particularly in high latitudes.

This suggests that two kinds of maps or charts existed during Mercator's time: the scholars' conical projection map and the navigators' plane chart. From Mercator's explanation it appears that plane charts were based on two different concepts: that of the distances and angles of the medieval compass chart, and that of Ptolemy's latitudes and longitudes.

Mercator's solution was accepted slowly, largely because he failed to explain his method of construction. The explanation in Edward Wright's *Certain Errors in Navigation* in 1594 helped, but nearly two centuries passed before Mercator's chart replaced the plane chart aboard ships.

PYL-KOMPAS

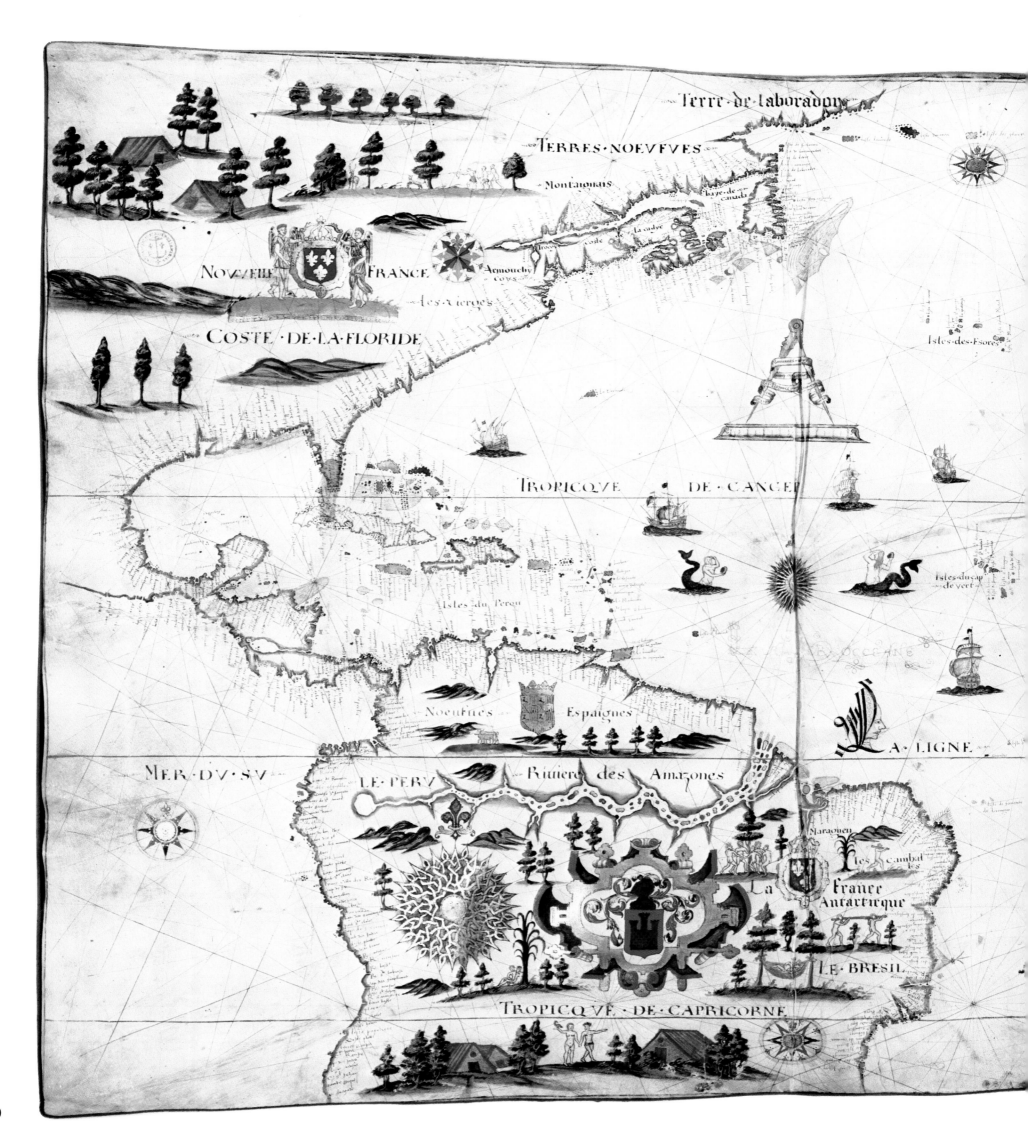

Terre de Laborador

TERRES·NOEVFVES

Montaignais

Nouvelle France

Coste de canada

la cadye

Armouchy cois

NOVVELLE FRANCE

des vierges

COSTE·DE·LA·FLORIDE

Isles des Esores

TROPICQVE DE·CANCER

Isles du cap de vert

Isles du Peron

OCCEANE

Noeufves Espaignes

LA·LIGNE

MER·DV·SV

LE·PERV

Riuiere des Amazones

Maragnen

Ies cambal les

La France Antartiqve

LE·BRESIL

TROPICQVE·DE·CAPRICORNE

PLATE 48
Portolano of the Atlantic
Ocean.
Pierre de Vaulx (Le Havre,
1613).
28⅜ x 42¹⁵/₁₆″, manuscript
on vellum.

The text in the title cartouche in the lower right of this particularly attractive chart of the Atlantic Ocean and the coasts of the lands bordering it, reads, *"Ceste carte A Este Faiste Au havre de Grace Par Pierre Devaulx Pilote Geographe Pour le Roy Ian 1613."* Pierre de Vaulx was a scion of a family of Normandy sailors and was, like his elder brother, Jacques, a pilot and chart maker working in the port of Le Havre.

With its decorative wind roses, scales of distances, ships, and mermaids in the water parts and scenes in the land parts—in particular the paradisaical representations in the South American continent—this chart is a feast for the spectator. It is also of interest because of the French claims to the North American mainland it justifies. The land is denoted as French—in the middle of the continent is depicted the French coat-of-arms with the three lilies and with the text *Nouvelle France* (New France). The English pretensions to the same area are ignored, and the chart thus foretells the English-French rivalry over this continent for the next two centuries.

The French claim on Guyana is indicated with the French coat-of-arms and the legend *La France Antarticque*. The chart has a latitude scale but no longitude scale. In those days the longitudinal position of a ship at sea could not be determined.

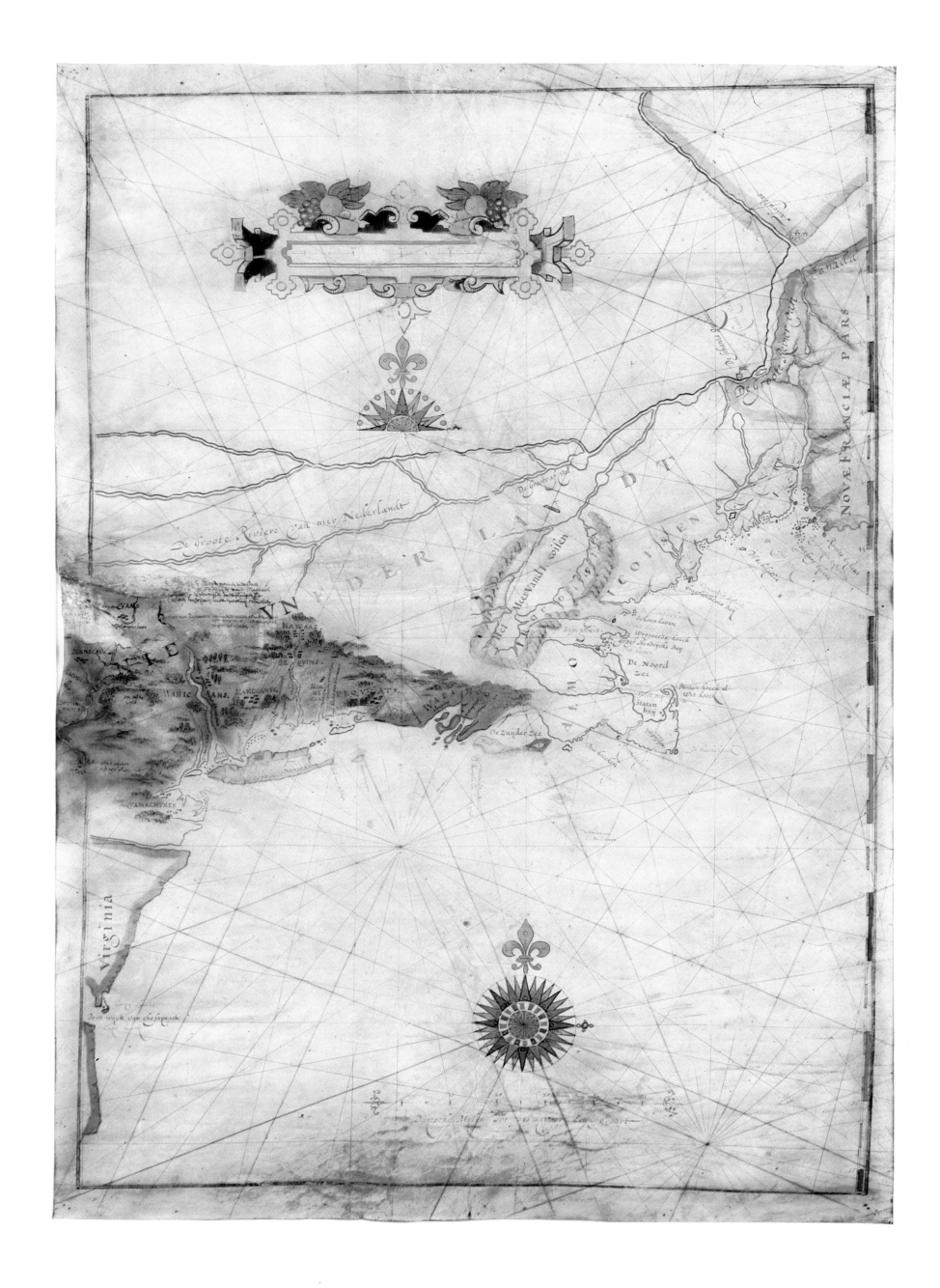

NOVÆ FRANCIÆ PARS

De groote af val

De groote Riviere van nieu Nederlandt

NV NEDERLANDT

Het Meerwandt wolsen

De Noord Zee

De Zuyder Zee

Virginia

De inwyck van Chesapeack

92

PLATE 49
Chart of the east coast of
America near New York.
Cornelius Doetsz (Edam,
1614).
24¹³⁄₁₆ x 16¾″, manuscript
on vellum.

The so-called Adriaen Block chart, dated 1614, is the earliest known chart depicting the area around present-day New York and of historical importance for the early history of this city. After the Englishman Henry Hudson, searching the Northwest Passage to China in the service of the Dutch, had surveyed the Hudson River, Dutch interest in the possibilities of fur trade with the Indians in this area was aroused. Other expeditions sailed from Holland with the instruction to investigate the possibilities of the fur trade and to survey the area. In the winter and spring of 1613/14 a number of ships under the command of the merchant Adriaen Block sailed in these parts and charted the area between Chesapeake Bay and Penobscot Bay.

Block had an important reason for his actions. In 1613 the States General of the Dutch Republic had decided that whoever would chart the area around the Hudson River would be granted the exclusive rights of trade in this area. Thus Block and his fellow merchants, united in the Company of Nieuw Nederland, were granted the exclusive rights of trade. This charter of the States General specifically mentions this chart, and for this reason it is of great historical importance for the history of the founding of New York.

The chart on vellum is for the most part drawn in red ink, with further elaboration of the Hudson River area in black ink. The following explanation can be given for this. Adriaen Block sailed from Holland at the end of 1613 with the still-uncompleted chart by the hand of the deceased Cornelis Doetsz, who had died earlier that year. This chart, drawn in red ink, was based upon the material gathered in previous expeditions in 1611 and 1612. After Block's return in 1614 it was amended in black ink. In the land part, Indian names like Nahican (Long Island) and Manhattan are drawn; in the sea part, Dutch names are given like *de Zuyderzee*, near Nantucket, *Staten hoeck*, for Cape Cod, and *de Noordzee*.

Cornelis Doetsz is one of the late sixteenth-century Dutch chart makers, part of the School of Edam, named after the small town of Edam on the border of the former Zuiderzee.

Johannes Janssonius was the lifetime rival of the Blaeus. Unlike Willem Blaeu, who started his career as a seller of sea charts, Johannes Janssonius's main interest never lay in the field of hydrographic publications; with only one exception he contented himself with a lesser role.

After the death of Jodocus Hondius in 1612, Hendrik Hondius, his son, together with his brother-in-law Janssonius, continued to publish the *Mercator-Hondius Atlas*, containing maps of the known world. When the plates of this atlas came into Willem Blaeu's possession, Hondius-Janssonius had new copies cut. In constant competition with the Blaeu firm, this atlas developed into the *Atlas Novus*, published for the first time in 1638. The outstanding feat of Janssonius in the hydrographic field is that he enlarged this *Atlas Novus* in 1650 by adding a fifth volume, a sea atlas named the *Water-Weerelt*. This was the first sea atlas—a collection of charts in folio size to serve as a general-purpose atlas—published in the Dutch Republic; all previous publications had been pilot guides. He was followed by other publishers of pilot books, for example Hendrik Doncker in 1659 and Pieter Goos in 1666. The chart of the Arctic regions is from this sea atlas. It is a polar stereographic projection chart.

As explained before, the Mercator projection cannot be used for depicting the poles, thus the stereographic projection method has to be used. The earth's surface is projected onto a plane perpendicular to the axis of the earth, just touching the pole. The opposed pole is the center of projection. The meridians in the chart are straight lines radiating from the center (the pole) of the chart; the parallels are circles with the pole as their center; and their mutual distance remains constant; its only drawback is that a course line cannot be drawn as a straight line.

The chart shows the discoveries in the northern regions of the Americas made in the first half of the seventeenth century by John Davis, William Baffin, Henry Hudson, and others in

PLATE 50
Chart of the North Pole.
Johannes Janssonius
(Amsterdam, 1650).
17⅛ x 21⅝″, copper
engraving on paper.
From the sea atlas *Atlantis
Majoris, Quinta Pars, Orbis
Maritimus.*

94

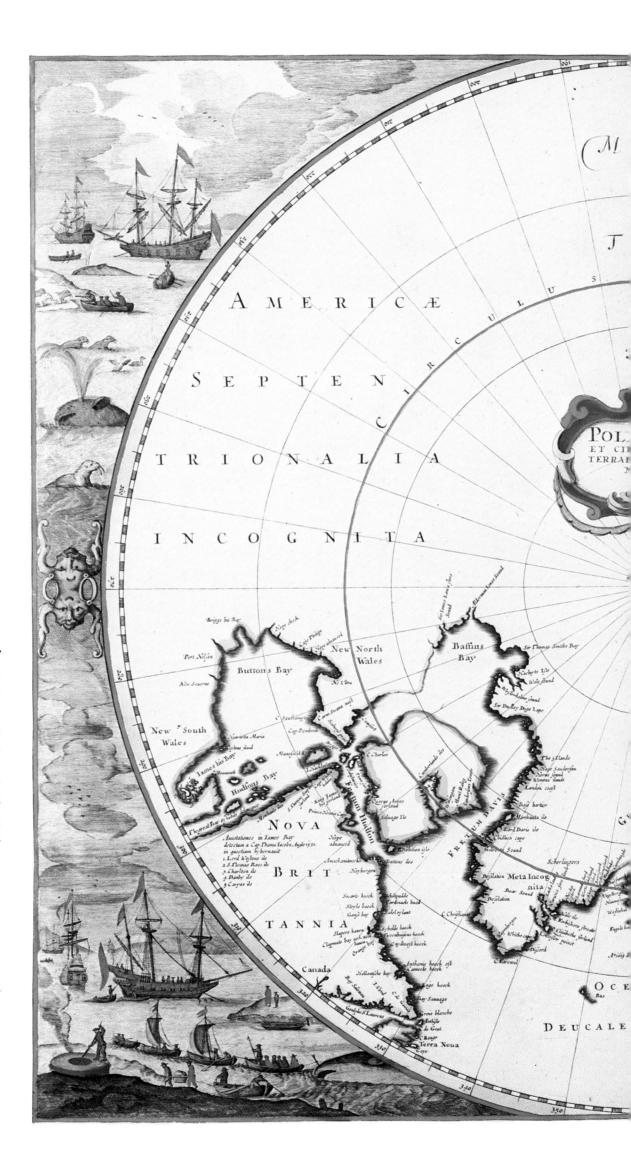

their search for the Northwest Passage to China. In the Arctic regions of Europe are depicted the results of Dutch explorations at the end of the sixteenth century. The chart is decorated with scenes of whale fishing in the four corners.

In the Mercator projection chart the North Pole cannot be depicted. For this reason Gerard Mercator showed the North Pole separately in his world chart of 1569. This depiction of the North Pole can be traced to the writings of Marco Polo at the end of the thirteenth century, which described the North Pole as a rock surrounded by water from four rivers. This was the traditional view until the Dutchman Willem Barentsz made his famous chart of the North Pole of 1598 showing open water.

PLATE 51
Chart of the North Pole.
Gerard Mercator (Duisburg, 1569).
17¾ x 11⁷⁄₁₆", copper engraving on paper.
Part of the world chart in Mercator projection.

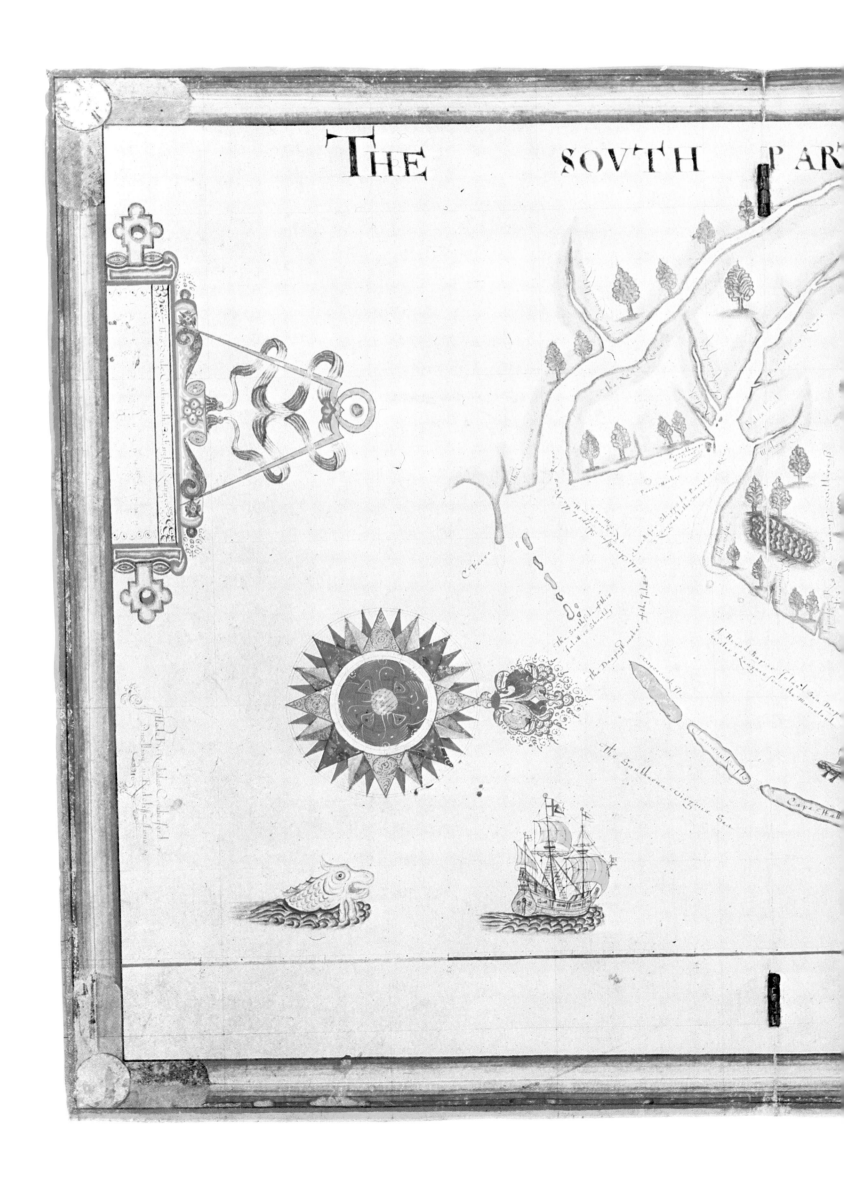

THE   SOVTH   PART

Little is known of Nicolas Comberford except that he was apprenticed as plate maker in the Draper's Company by John Daniell in the years between 1612 and 1620 and that he worked in Ratcliffe. He belongs to the Thames School of chart makers, together with other cartographers like John Daniell, John Burston, John Thornton, Andre Welch, and Joel Cascoyne. The large-scale chart depicts the waters of the Pamlico and Albemarle sounds on the Atlantic coast of North America. It was there in 1524 that Verrazano thought that he had found an entrance to the Pacific.

The chart has a certain naive charm, with the trees and the animals illustrating the land, while the ship, the fish, and the two men in the rowboat decorate the water.

Like many of the charts of the Thames School, Comberford's manuscript chart, drawn on vellum, is mounted on two hinged oak boards.

PLATE 52
Portolano of North Carolina, Albemarle, and Pamlico Sound.
Nicholas Comberford (London, 1657).
38 x 50", manuscript on vellum, pasted on two hinged boards.

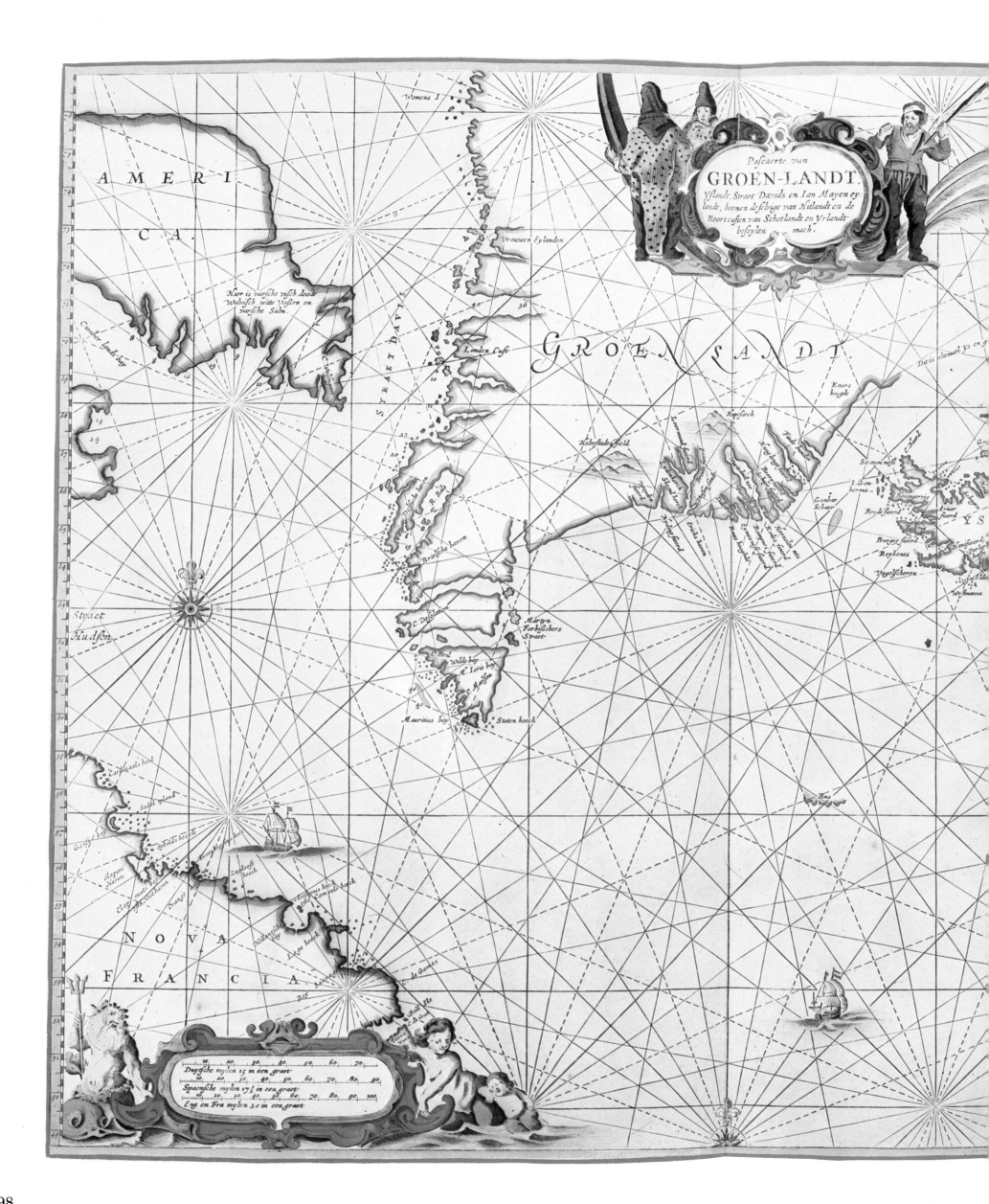

AMERICA

CA.

GROENLANDT

Straet Davids

Straet
Hudson

NOVA

FRANCIA

Womeus I.

Vrouwen Eylanden

Hier is varsche visch door
Walvisch witte Vossen en
varsche Salm.

Londen Lust

Dit is alemael Ys en g

Koors
hoogde

Hapsarck

Helmstade sield

Dolpsche haven
R. Rols

Brielsche haven

C. Desolation

Martyn
Forbisschers
Strat

C. Bril
Wilde bay
Mr Ioris bay
C. Maessu

M aurisius bay   Staten hoeck

Ysland

Reykenes

Vogelscheren

Westmana

Bus

Carthaels hod

Sadel eyland

Spitolds hoeck

Stagers
haven

Orangie

Leegen hoeck

Le Gentus

C. Bali Ile

Pascaerte van
GROEN-LANDT,
Yslandt, Straet Davids en Ian Mayen ey-
landt, hoemen de schiope van Hitlandt en de
Noort custen van Schotlandt en Vrlandt
beseylen mach.

Duytsche mylen 15 in een graet
10   20   30   40   50   60   70   80   90
Spaensche mylen 17½ in een graet
10   20   30   40   50   60   70   80   90   100
Eng en Fra mylen 20 in een graet

98

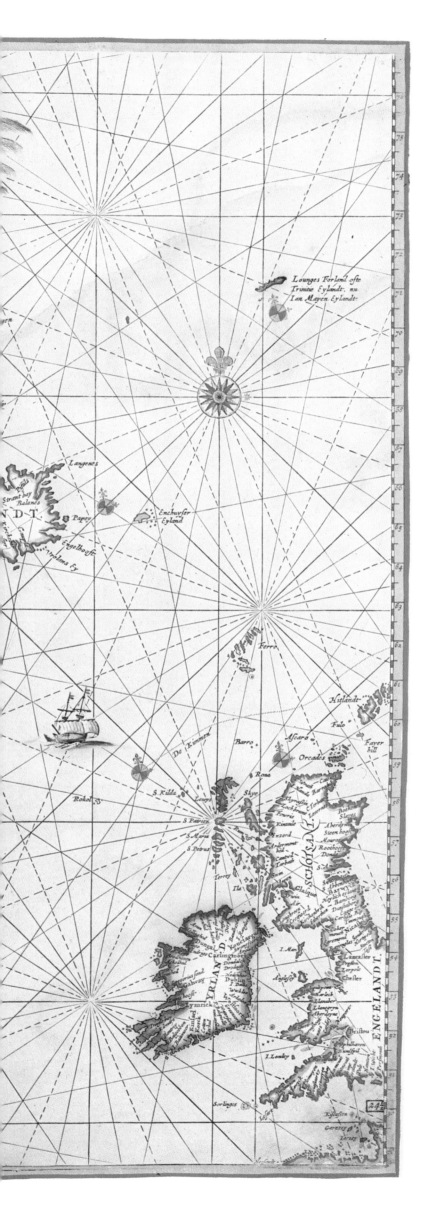

PLATE 53
Sea chart of the seas around
Greenland and Iceland.
Pieter Goos (Amsterdam,
1666).
16¹⁵⁄₁₆ x 20½", copper
engraving on paper.
From the atlas *The Sea
Atlas of the Water World.*

Dᵁʳⁱⁿᵍ Holland's Golden Age in the seventeenth century, Pieter Goos was one of Amsterdam's most prominent publishers of nautical charts. The reputation of his firm was matched only by that of the publishing houses of Blaeu and van Keulen. Like most of his contemporaries, Goos's shop, named "In the Golden Sea Mirror" was located near the waterfront of the Dutch capital, the Ij. Ships from all parts of the world moored there while their crews resupplied and their navigators purchased charts and instruments such as compasses and Jacob's staffs.

In 1650 Goos published a pilot guide entitled the *Zeespiegel (Sea Mirror)*, which contained charts of the seacoasts of the "Northern, Eastern and Western Navigation." Although it was not an original work, it remained in print for some twenty-eight years. During that time, there were few changes in its original text, but it was expanded in 1662 to include the *Straatsboeck*, containing twenty-five charts of the Mediterranean area. For this, the publisher copied charts initially issued by Theunisz Jacobsz's sons, Jacob T'eunisz and Caspar Lootsman. Goos's renown was that he was the first to propose adding a fourth and a fifth section to the pilot guide. These contained charts of the Atlantic coastal waters bordering Africa and America. The fourth section was based on the second part of Arent Roggeveen's *Het Brandend Veen*, with charts and sailing directions for the West African coast down to the Cape of Good Hope. For unknown reasons, this was not published until 1865 by Jacob Robijn, who had obtained the plates. The fifth part, which appeared shortly before Goos's death in 1675, included thirty-three charts of Guyana, the Caribbean, and the North American coast as far north as Newfoundland. As such, Goos's work was the forerunner of the *Zeefakkel (Sea Torch)*, the famous pilot guide in five parts published by Johannes van Keulen.

In 1666, sixteen years after first publishing his pilot guide, Goos published the *Sea Atlas of the Water World*, which was a copy of Hendrik Doncker's atlas of the same name. Comprising some forty nautical charts, this book remained unchanged during Goos's lifetime. Goos, the copier, was also copied by others. The charts of John Seller's *The English Pilot*, initially issued in 1671/72, were taken primarily from Goos's work.

As a publisher, Goos had more shipowners and officials among his clientele than did his competitors. Consequently, his sea atlases, with their wide-bordered charts on thick paper, are found relatively often even now. The pilot guides used aboard ships are much scarcer, even though they were printed in much larger quantities.

After Goos's death, his widow, together with his son Hendrik, published a few editions with forty-four charts. Some exceptionally beautiful examples of these works, hand-colored and highlighted with gold by talented artists, were

sold by the famous Amsterdam publisher Albert Magnus.

Pieter Goos's decorative sea chart (plate 53) depicts the seas near Greenland. Irish monks were the first to visit Greenland—still uninhabited—around 764. In 867 the Norseman Nadd-Odd was swept up onto Greenland's coast, and seven years later the first colony of Norsemen was established. In 983 Eric the Red reached Greenland and two years later sailed around Greenland's southernmost point; in the chart it is called "Staten Hoek." From Greenland the Norsemen reached the American continent around the year 1000.

The Norse settlements had long since vanished when Martin Frobisher reached Greenland in 1576 in his search for a Northwest Passage to China. In 1585/87 John Davis scouted the coast of the strait that has since borne his name. The legend in present-day Baffin Island reads: "Here is fresh fish, dead whales, white foxes and fresh salmon."

The chart taken from Goos's *Sea Atlas* depicts the area between present-day New York and the Delaware Bay. Staten Island and Manhattan are more or less correctly drawn, but Long Island is not depicted as an island.

As early as 1614 (six years before the Pilgrims landed), Dutch merchants had established a trading center—Fort Nassau—near what is now Albany, New York, but they were more interested in fur trade than in colonization. The first true settlements were started by the Dutch West Indies Company at Fort Orange (1624) and Fort Amsterdam (1625). The latter was on Manhattan Island, which in 1626 Governor Pieter Minuit bought from the Indians for sixty guilders—then twenty-four dollars—worth of merchandise. In 1664, a subsequent governor, Peter Stuyvesant, was forced to surrender New Amsterdam to the English fleet, and the city was renamed New York in honor of the duke of York, brother of the English king. The Dutch recaptured the territory in 1673 but gave it back to the English the following year in exchange for Surinam.

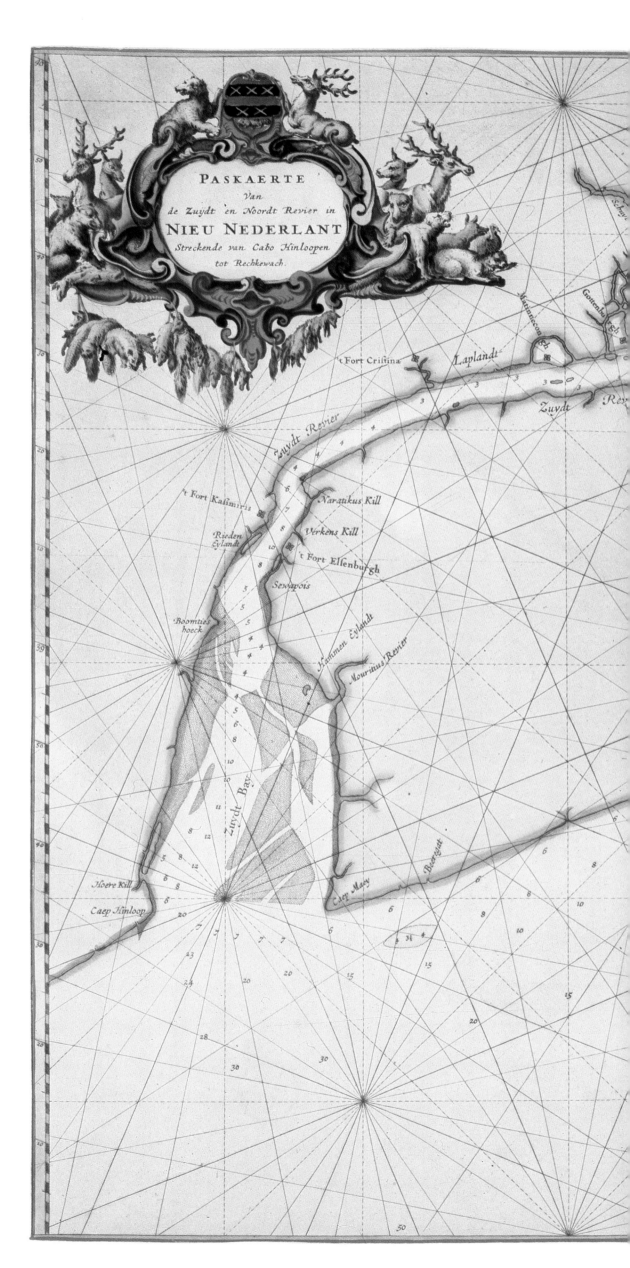

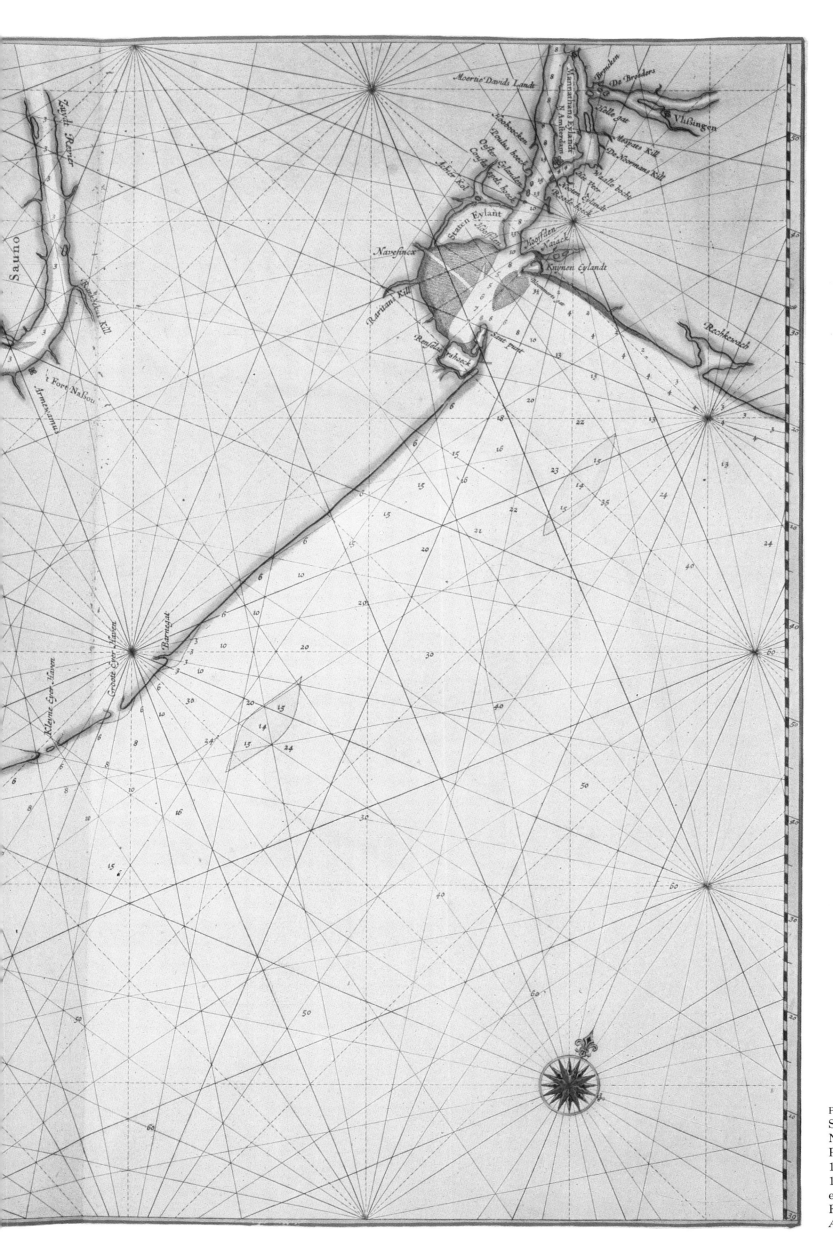

PLATE 54
Sea chart of the coast near
New York.
Pieter Goos (Amsterdam,
1666).
19⅞ x 23⅝″, copper
engraving on paper.
From the atlas *The Sea
Atlas of the Water World*.

101

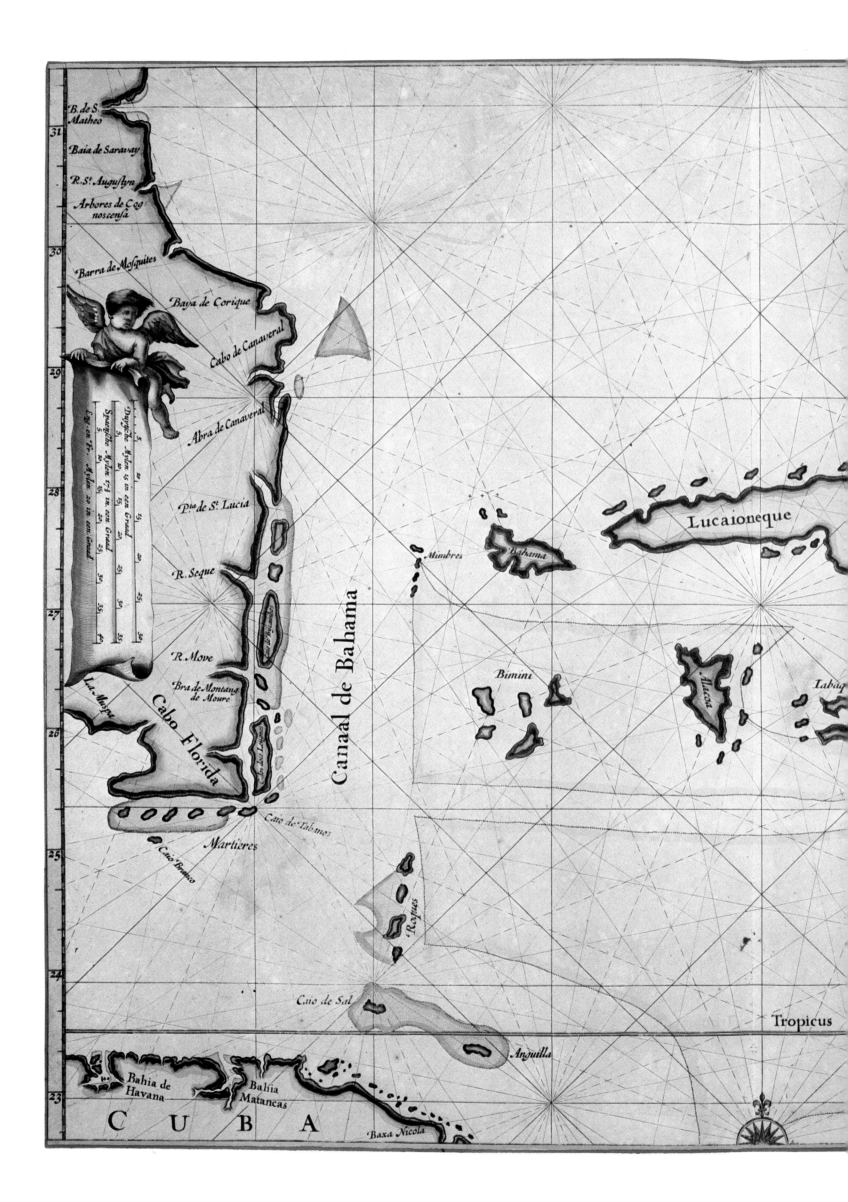

B. de S.
Matheo

Baia de Saravay

R. St. Augustyn

Arbores de Cog-
noscensa

Barra de Mosquites

Baya de Corique

Cabo de Canaveral

Abra de Canaveral

P.ta de St. Lucia

R. Seque

R. Move

Bra. de Montang.
de Moure

Lae Mosru

Cabo Florida

Cato de Tabtmo

Caio Branco

Martieres

Canaal de Bahama

Mimbres

Bahama

Lucaioneque

Bimini

Maccu

Tabaq

Roques

Caio de Sal

Anguilla

Tropicus

Bahia de
Havana

Bahia
Matancas

Baxa Nicola

C U B A

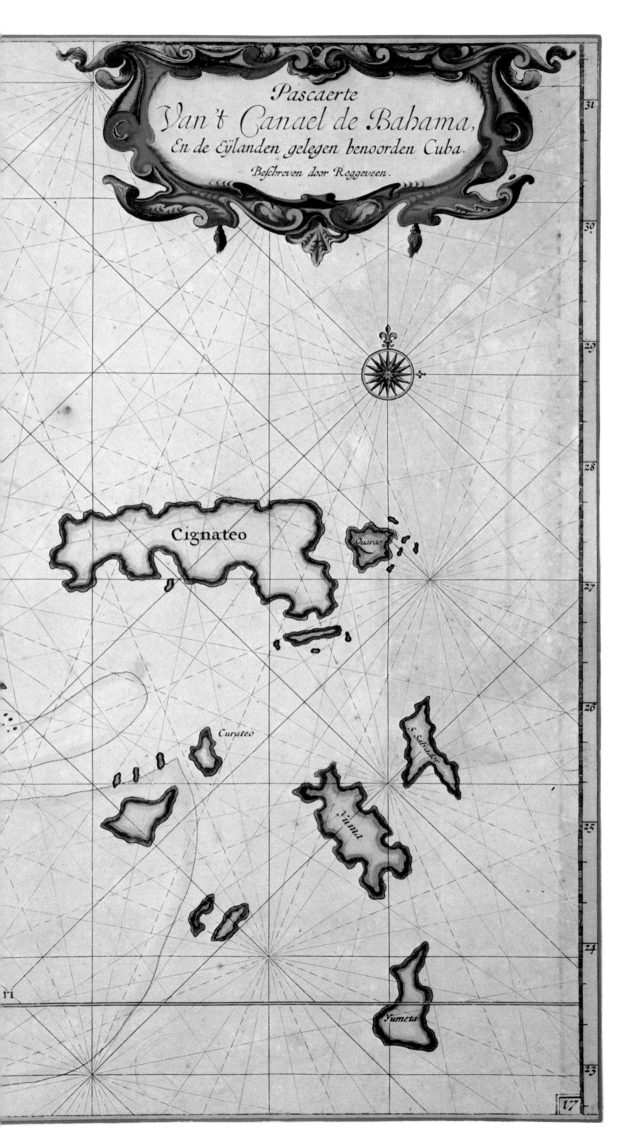

PLATE 55
Sea chart of the coast of
Florida.
Arent Roggeveen and
Pieter Goos (Amsterdam,
1675).
15¹⁵/₁₆ x 20¼", copper
engraving on paper.
From the sea atlas *The
Burning Fen, Part One.*

In order to reach the comparatively safe Atlantic, homeward-bound Spanish armadas had
to sail through the dangerous rock-strewn area
of the Bahamas. At first they sailed from Havana in an eastern direction along Cuba's north
coast and through the Old Bahama Channel, a
dangerous corridor only twenty-five miles wide.
Later the treasure fleets passed through the
wider New Bahama Channel located between
Florida's east coast and Little Bahama Bank.

The heavily loaded galleons were unwieldy,
and the combined hazards of hurricanes and
treacherous reefs turned the Bahamas into a
ships' graveyard. But nature was not the only
threat to the treasure-laden vessels of the armadas. The innumerable shoals, reefs, and channels of the area were ideal nests for buccaneers,
and many a galleon fell prey to the Bahama
pirates. From there Henry Morgan initiated his
raids on Cuba and the Spanish Main.

The chart of Arent Roggeveen depicts the east
coast of Florida north to Cape Canaveral. It was
scouted for the first time by Juan Ponce de Leon,
one of Columbus's companions, who searched for
the mythical island with the fountain of eternal
youth. Ponce de Leon did not find the fountain
but was the first to see the mighty Gulf Stream.

Arent Roggeveen taught the art of navigation
to the pilots of the Middelburg Chamber of both
the Dutch East and West Indies companies. In
this function he must have had access to the
companies' collections of "secret" charts of the
non-European waters. It is very likely that these

collections were the source of information for the two pilot guides Roggeveen compiled: one of the West African seas and the other of the coastal waters of Guyana, the Caribbean, and the east coast of North America up to Terra Nova. Pieter Goos planned to publish these pilot guides. Named *The Burning Fen*—referring to Roggeveen's name (*Veen* means "fen") a burning fen was used as a beacon for shipping—they were to have been the fourth and fifth part of his own pilot guide, *The Sea Mirror*.

Goos published only the part with the charts of the American coasts; he died shortly after its publication in 1675. It was not before 1685 that the part containing the charts of the West African seas was published by Jacob Robijn, who had obtained the charts from the Goos heirs. The reasons for this delay are unknown, but in the meantime Johannes van Keulen, Robijn's competitor, had published his very successful pilot guide, *The Sea Torch*, in five parts.

Arent Roggeveen was not only the first cartographer to compile a printed pilot guide of non-European waters, he also prepared an exploration to the southern Pacific. Although he obtained a grant for such a voyage from the States General of the United Provinces, he never sailed the unknown Terra Australis because he failed to raise sufficient financial support. However, his son Jacob succeeded where he had not. In 1721–22 Jacob crossed the Pacific, and discovered Easter Island with its mysterious idols.

PLATE 56
Map of the St. Lawrence River.
Jean Baptiste Louis Franquelin.
16⅛ x 81⅞″, manuscript on paper.

The first French attempt to colonize North America was made by Jacques Cartier (1491–1557). This mariner from St. Malo in Brittany made three voyages between 1534 and 1541, exploring the gulf and the St. Lawrence River in his search for the Northwest Passage.

In 1535 he sailed up the St. Lawrence River in Canada, past the rock of Quebec, past the Iroquois village he called Mont Real, until he reached the lowest rapids of the St. Lawrence. These rapids made him realize that his attempt to find a passage to China would not succeed. Because of this failure, and the apparent scarcity of precious metals and stones, the French lost interest in the territory and stopped all further attempts to colonize it.

During the second half of the sixteenth century French fishermen continued to visit the rich fishing grounds off the northeastern coast of America. Thus, trading contacts with the Indians were established. As the European demand for furs increased, the fur trade with the Indians became more and more important. At the beginning of the seventeenth century—when the religious wars in France had ceased—a second attempt at colonizing in this part of America was made. The voyage of Samuel de Champlain resulted in the establishment of a fur trade station at Quebec in 1600. Champlain further explored the St. Lawrence and the interior of North America, thus discovering the Ottawa River and the Great Lakes. In New France, as it was then known, the French succeeded against the Dutch and English in consolidating their interests in the fur trade.

The manuscript chart shown here is by the French "hydrographer to the king" Jean Baptiste Louis Franquelin (1653–c. 1725). It depicts the mouth of the St. Lawrence River and the river itself up to the Isle of Orleans, just downstream from Quebec.

INDIAN OCEAN

The oldest information about the lands around the Indian Ocean comes from the periplus (pilot guide) of Niarchus, an admiral of the fleet of Alexander the Great. He sailed from the Indus along the coast of Persia. Onesicritus, Niarchus's pilot, was the first to report the fabulous island of Taprobane (Ceylon), giving it too great a magnitude.

The periplus of the Erythraeian Sea—the Indian Ocean—written at the end of the first century, includes the northern end of the Red Sea and gives information about Africa's east coast as far as Zanzibar. It reports correctly that farther south the coast turns west and that the Indian and the Atlantic oceans meet. This information was soon replaced by Ptolemy's misinformation. His map shows Africa connected to Southeast Asia, making the Indian Ocean an inland sea. In the East the periplus reports the coast of Arabia, the entrance to the Persian Gulf, and the coasts of Persia and India to Muziris. From there, the writer relied on the information of others and became less accurate.

When Christopher Columbus returned from his voyage with reports about his putative discoveries on the east coast of Asia, the Portuguese understood that time was running out. Bartholomeu Dias had proved the confluence of the Atlantic and Indian oceans when he sailed around the Cape of Good Hope in 1486. By the king's orders in 1487 the Portuguese Covilha traveled overland to the kingdom of Malabar on the west coast of India, where he visited the important markets of Cannanore and Calicut. Both there, and in Hormuz, in the mouth of the Persian Gulf, he met merchants who told him exciting tales of the mysterious Spice Islands.

Such was the knowledge about the Asian coasts when Vasco da Gama departed on July 8, 1497, from Lisbon to become the first European to sail along Africa's coasts past the Cape of Good Hope, reaching Calicut on the Malabar coast in May 1498.

Within twenty years Portuguese discoveries added 100 degrees, or more than a quarter of the earth's surface, to the known world. In 1500 and 1506 Pedralvarez Cabral and Tristao da Cunha surveyed Africa's east coast up to the mouth of the Red Sea. In 1508 and 1513 the coasts of the Persian Gulf and of the Red Sea were charted. Ceylon was given its correct proportions, and in 1511 when Albequerque conquered Malacca —with Hormuz in the Persian Gulf and Calicut on the Malabar coast, the most important ports of commerce in the Asian waters—the base of Portuguese control in the Indian Ocean was established. It would last for almost a century.

From Malacca the Moluccas were visited for the first time in 1512, as was China after 1514.

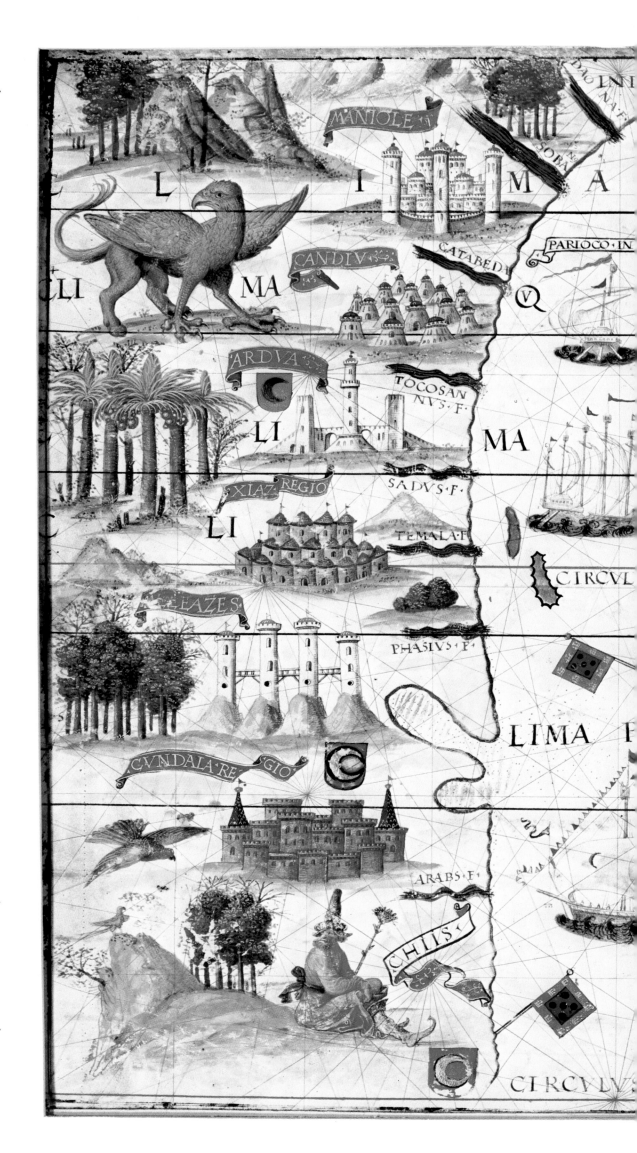

PLATE 57
Portolano of the Chinese
coast near Shanghai—
Magnus Golfus Chinarum.
Lopo Homem and Pedro and

Jorge Reinel (Lisbon,
1518–19).
16½ x 23⁷⁄₁₆", manuscript
on vellum.
From an untitled atlas.

The coast of New Guinea was explored, and, perhaps, the west coast of Australia.

The era of Portuguese discoveries in the East came to an end when Japan was visited by a Portuguese ship in 1542. An imperium was built that lasted until they were displaced by the Dutch in the seventeenth century.

The island of Chu-san was a free port where the Chinese allowed the Portuguese to negotiate the trade between China and Japan. These two countries were enemies for centuries. An attempted invasion of Japan in 1284 by the Mongol conquerer Kublai Khan, emperor of China at whose court Marco Polo stayed for many years, was shattered at the last moment by the "divine winds" or "Kamikaze." However, Japan was dependent on China for the production of silk, while China wanted the silver dug in Japan. Each country forbade the other's ships to enter its ports and for this reason an intermediary was necessary. This enormous and profitable transshipment enterprise was handled by the Portuguese from the moment they entered these waters.

The portolano depicted here belongs, like the chart of Brazil (plate 10), to an atlas made by the Portuguese cartographers Lopo Homen and father and son Pedro and Jorge Reinel in the years 1518–19. It was probably intended to give the French king Francis I an impression of the vastness of Portugal's possessions outside of Europe.

The chart gives a symbolic representation of the Gulf of Shanghai, the *Magnus Golfus Chinarum*.

Next to the Portuguese merchant, recognizable by the crosses on its sails, the chart shows Chinese ships with five and six masts. When Marco Polo returned from China, escorting a Chinese princess on her way to Persia, he sailed with fourteen ships, each with four masts and a crew of 200 mariners or more.

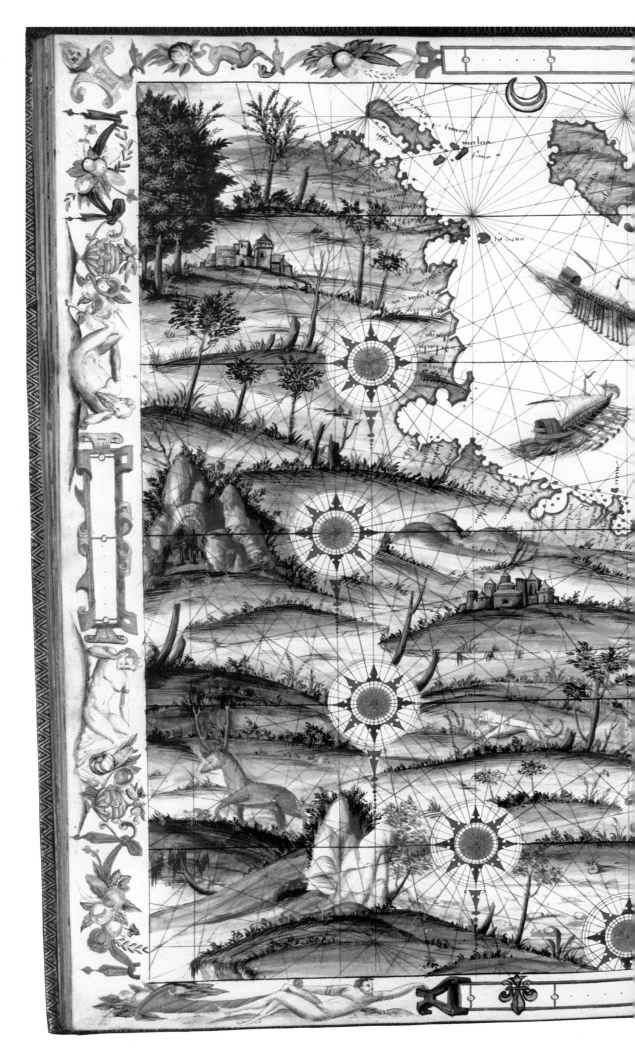

From representations of vessels found in the graves of the Egyptians we know the type of ships that sailed the Red Sea at the time of the pharaohs. Pliny, the Roman historian, tells us about the trade route from Alexandria to the Far East. After the goods were brought by ship as far up the Nile as possible, they were unloaded and carried across the desert to the port of Berenice, on the African coast of the Red Sea. From there the Roman merchant ships sailed to the port of Ocelis at the mouth of the Red Sea; the trip took thirty days. The preserved periplus of the Erythraeian Sea, written in the first century A.D. by an Alexandrian merchant, gives a description of the African coast of the Red Sea from the port of Berenice to Cape Guardafui.

The Arabs conquered Egypt in 638 and the Red Sea became an Arabian inland sea. It was the Arabs who, after the fall of the eastern Roman Empire, kept safe and enlarged the geographical knowledge of the Greeks. After the death of the prophet Mohammed, they built a vast empire, encompassing Spain in the west and a large part of Asia in the east. But they were also keen merchants, and they ventured beyond China to the Russian plains and the borders of the Baltic; in the south they traveled to Madagascar, off the east coast of Africa.

During the Crusades, starting at the end of the eleventh century, Europeans came in contact with Arab civilization and Arab translations of the works of the Greeks; these were in turn translated into Latin. In this way the knowledge

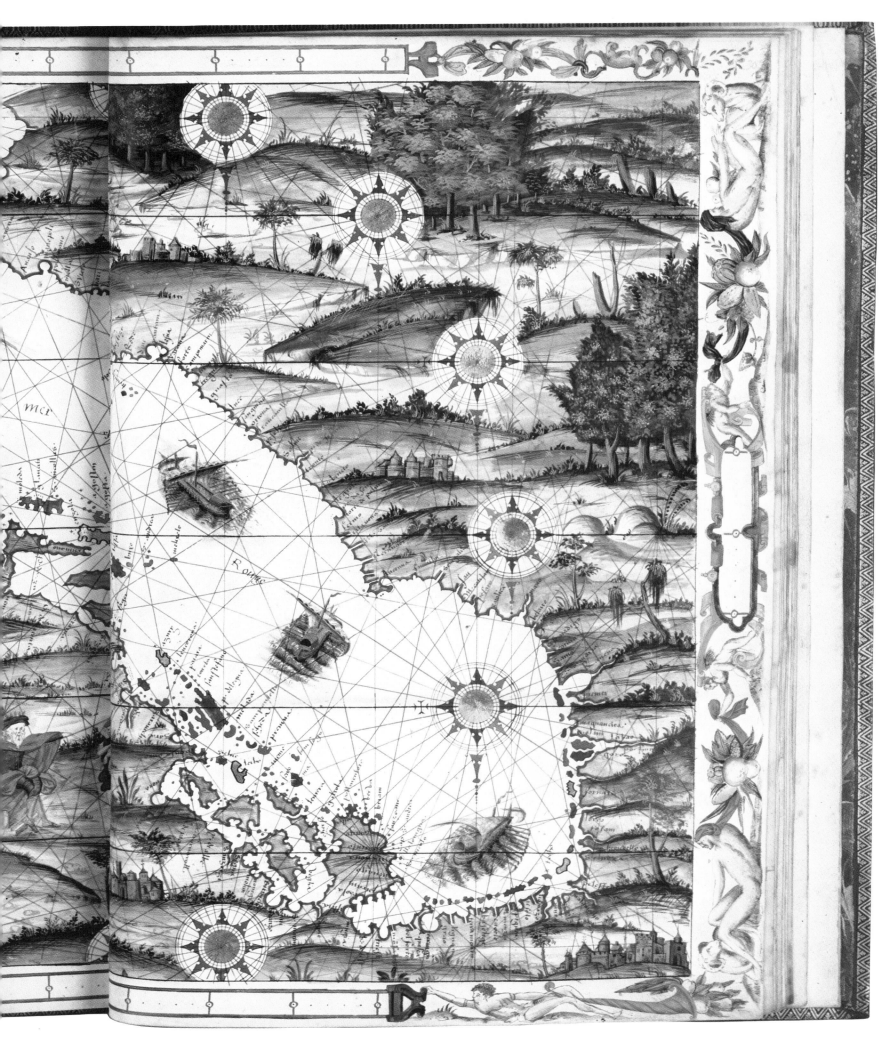

of the classical geographers came to modern Europe.

The Arabs were the mercantile representatives between Europe and the Far East until the Portuguese opened the trade route to the Orient via the Cape of Good Hope at the end of the fifteenth century.

The Red Sea was frequently navigated for another reason: for centuries Islamic pilgrims sailed to the port of Jidda en route to their holy city, Mecca. This chart is part of an atlas made by an anonymous Portuguese cartographer working around 1538 in the French port Dieppe. The Portuguese knowledge of the Red Sea dates from 1513 when it was navigated and charted by order of the Portuguese conquistador Alfonso d'Albequerque. The decorative elements in the land parts and the borders are by a French hand.

PLATE 58
Portolano of the Red Sea.
Anonymous, School of
Dieppe (Dieppe, c. 1538).
16½ x 24¹³⁄₁₆″, manuscript
on vellum.
From an untitled atlas.

PLATE 59
Sea chart of the coasts of
Northeast Asia.
Gerard Mercator (Duisburg,
1569).
15⁹⁄₁₆ x 24¹³⁄₁₆″, copper
engraving on paper.
Part of Gerard Mercator's
world chart.

Besides intending to construct a chart that ful-
filled the requirements of long-distance navigation, Mercator aimed to represent as accurately
as possible all the continents and waters of the
world. His extensive reading is well known, and
he based his chart upon the works of the classical writers Claudius Ptolemy, Pomponius Mela,
and Pliny; upon the itinerary of the putative
voyage of the Zeno brothers to Northern America; upon Marco Polo's writings about Asia; and
on biblical tales and medieval legends. In addition to these sources he used the information

gathered by his Spanish and Portuguese contemporaries. He was a child of the era between the
old and the new. Of necessity, the reliability of
the information depended upon the then-existing
knowledge of the various parts of the world.

Tartary and the regions of the North Pole
were then for the most part *terra incognita*. On
Mercator's chart of the *Oceanus Scythicus* or *Mare
Tabin* and the northeastern part of Asia we read
the names of the biblical Gog and Magog who,
as later legends tell, were ousted by Alexander
the Great and imprisoned until Judgment Day

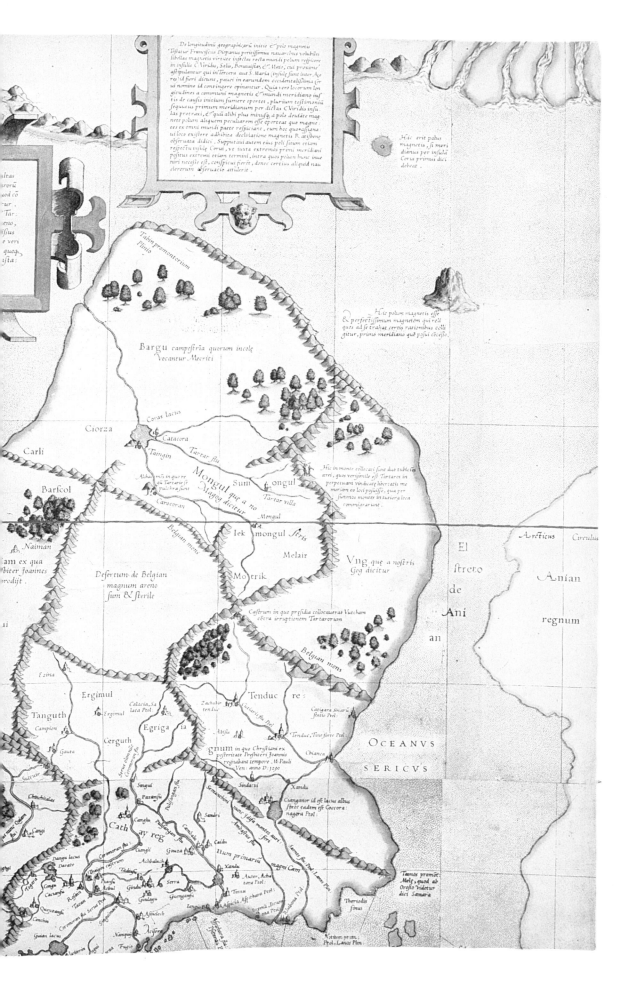

behind an iron wall on the peninsula beyond the Caspian gates. When that day arrived, they and their companions in evil were to overrun the civilized world. Mercator also placed the kingdom of Prester John in this part of the world, in contrast to its customary position in East Africa, in what is now Ethiopia.

Mercator also based his chart on Jacob Cnoyen's *Inventio Fortunatae*. At the upper left one sees the delta of the river that sprang through a rock in the water surrounding the North Pole and streamed into the Tabin Sea. In one of the

legends in the chart Mercator described the world according to the writers of antiquity. On the northern regions of Europe and Asia the legend reads:

The remainder of the northern boundary after crossing the Riphei Mountains is decribed by Pliny and on the left hand shore of the Scythian Ocean, he discusses Norway, Sweden and Finland under the names of Balthia, Basilia, Scandinavia and Eningia in Bk. 4, chapt. 13, but he described them as islands for he was unaware of the isthmus which separates the Gulf of Finland from Grandvic. Then, following the right hand shore in Bk. 6, chapt. 13, he places first, after the Hyperborean nations, Lytarmis, a promontory of Mount Rypheus, then the Arimpheans and most of the other nations who dwell around the Caspian Sea and it mouths, in fact he believed that it flowed into the Scythian Ocean; thence, having enumerated and described, in chapt. 17, the position and the peoples of the rest of the shore, he rounds Cape Tabis and arrives at the Serae by that side of the shores which faces the summer sunrise.

The northeastern extremity, *Tabin promontorium Plinio* is the cape that mariners had to round in order to pass through the mythical "Strait of Anian" to reach the China Sea. This idea, depicted here by Mercator, played an important role in the endeavors of the English and, at the end of the sixteenth century of the Dutch to reach the lands of Southeast Asia by way of this passage.

Once the icebergs around Novaja Zeml'a had been passed, the mariner would find open water and, after rounding Cape Tabin, encounter the Pacific and the riches of the Spice Islands.

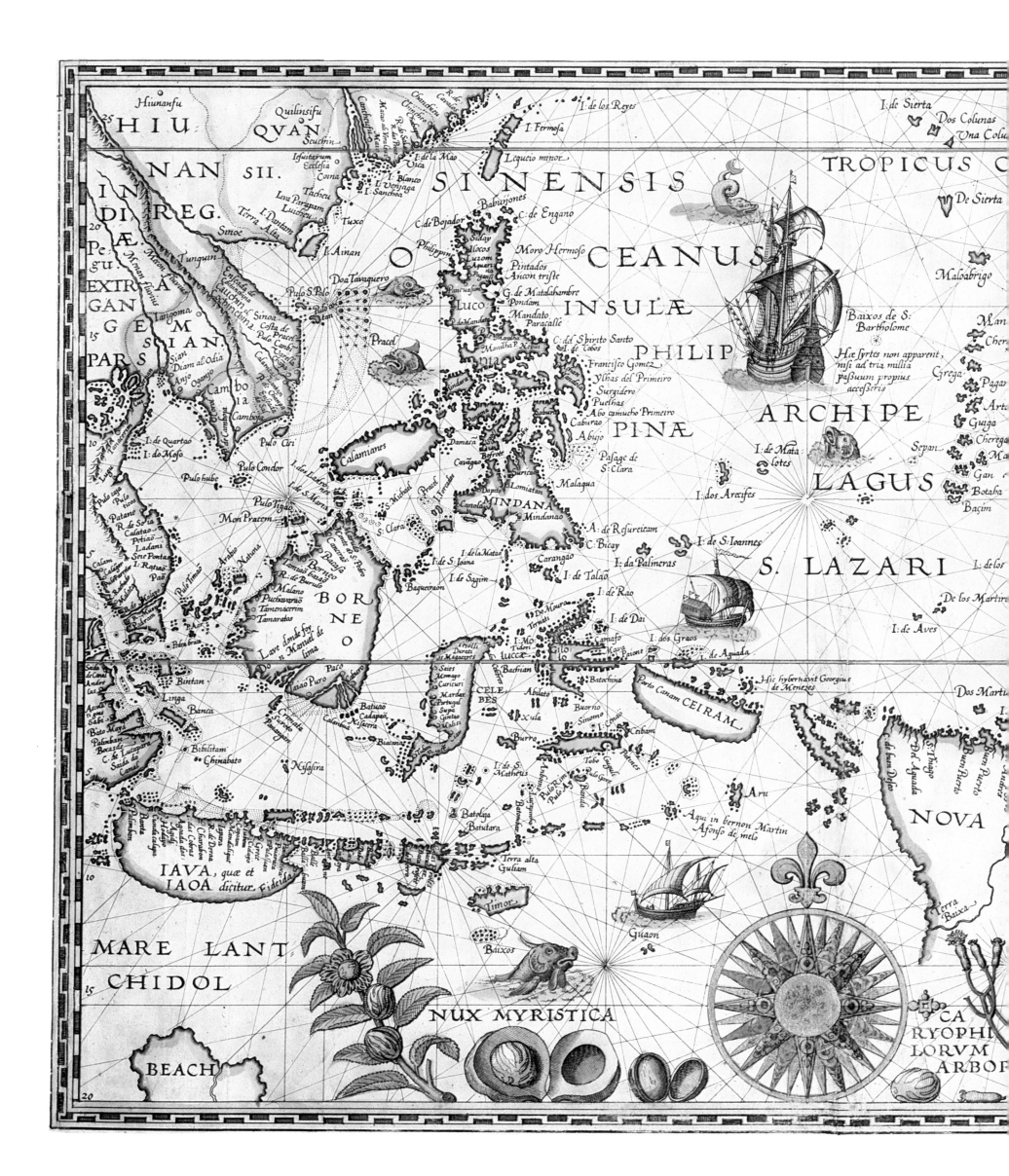

HIU QVAN

Hiunanfu
Quilinfifu
Scutbin

NAN SII.

IN DI REG.

Pe gu.

EXTRI GAN GEM SIAN.

PARS

Tunquin

Sinoe

Camboia

SINENSIS

OCEANUS

INSULÆ

PHILIP

PINÆ

TROPICUS C

De Sierta

Maloabrigo

Baixos de S. Bartholome

Hæ syrtes non apparent, nifi ad tria millia paßuum propius accefseris

ARCHIPE

LAGUS

S. LAZARI

BORNEO

CALAMIANES

MINDANA
Mindanao

Malaqua

CELE BES

CEIRAM

Hic hybernauit Georgius de Menezes

NOVA

IAVA, quæ et IAOA dicitur.

MARE LANT CHIDOL

Timor

Guaon

Baixos

Aqui in hernou Martin Afonso de melo

Aru

Terra Baixa

BEACH

NUX MYRISTICA

CA RYOPHI LORVM ARBOR

Because of religious persecution, Petrus Plancius left the southern Netherlands and accepted an invitation to work in Amsterdam. He was not only a theologian but also an accomplished cartographer and mathematician. Plancius played an important role in preparing all the voyages of discovery attempted by the Dutch around the turn of the century. He was the scientific expert for the voyage to the East Indies undertaken by Cornelis de Houtman between 1595 and 1597. From a commercial point of view this was not a very successful journey, but it yielded important information about navigation to the East Indies. Plancius included this information in his charts. When a Dutch fleet of eight ships under the command of Jacob Cornelisz van Neck left Holland for the East Indies in 1598, the pilots had at their disposal Plancius's world chart based on the Mercator projection. It is likely that Plancius's charts were the first charts in Mercator projection actually used aboard ships. He made some other Mercator charts, including one of the Mediterranean. Unfortunately none of these charts exist today. The Dutch East Indies Company was organized in 1602, and Plancius became the first cartographer of the company, a post he held until his death in 1622.

Plancius's chart of the Moluccas is based on the work of the Portuguese cartographer Bartholomeu Lasso. Lasso, who passed an examination in 1570 that entitled him to make and sell sea charts and nautical instruments, sold his charts to the Dutch despite the Portuguese embargo on such material.

The Amsterdam printer Cornelis Claesz obtained twenty-five sea charts from Bartholomeu Lasso through negotiations with Petrus Plancius. Plancius used these charts to compile his own charts, and for that reason Lasso's influence on Dutch cartography was considerable. As Plancius was the first hydrographer to the Dutch East Indies Company, his chart became the standard for seventeenth-century Dutch charting of the Indian Archipelago.

Engraved by the master engraver Johannes Doeticum, the chart shows the products of the archipelago: nutmeg, cloves, and several kinds of sandalwood.

PLATE 60
Sea chart of Malacca, the
Indonesian Archipelago, and
the Philippines.
Petrus Plancius
(Amsterdam, c. 1595).
15⁹/₁₆ x 21⁷/₈″, copper
engraving on paper.

113

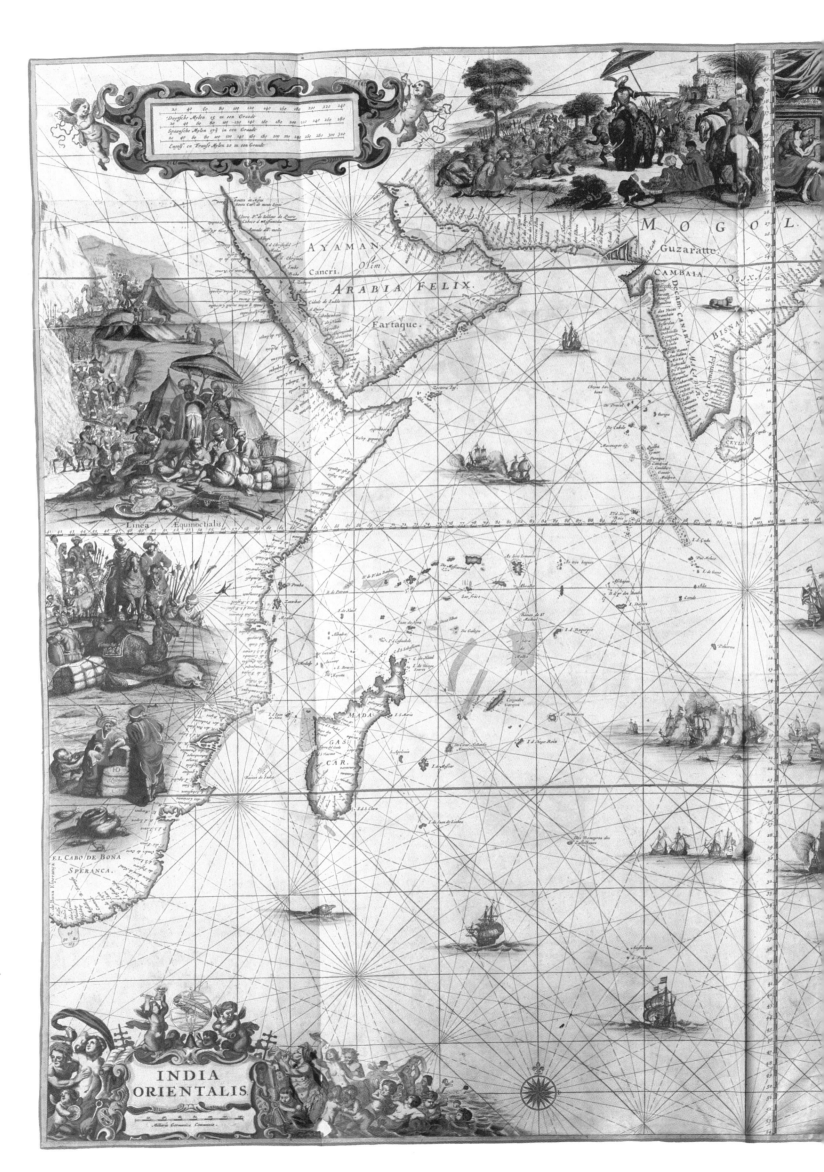

PLATE 61
Sea chart of the Indian
Ocean.
Hendrik Doncker
(Amsterdam).
29⅛ x 36¼″, copper
engraving on paper.

114

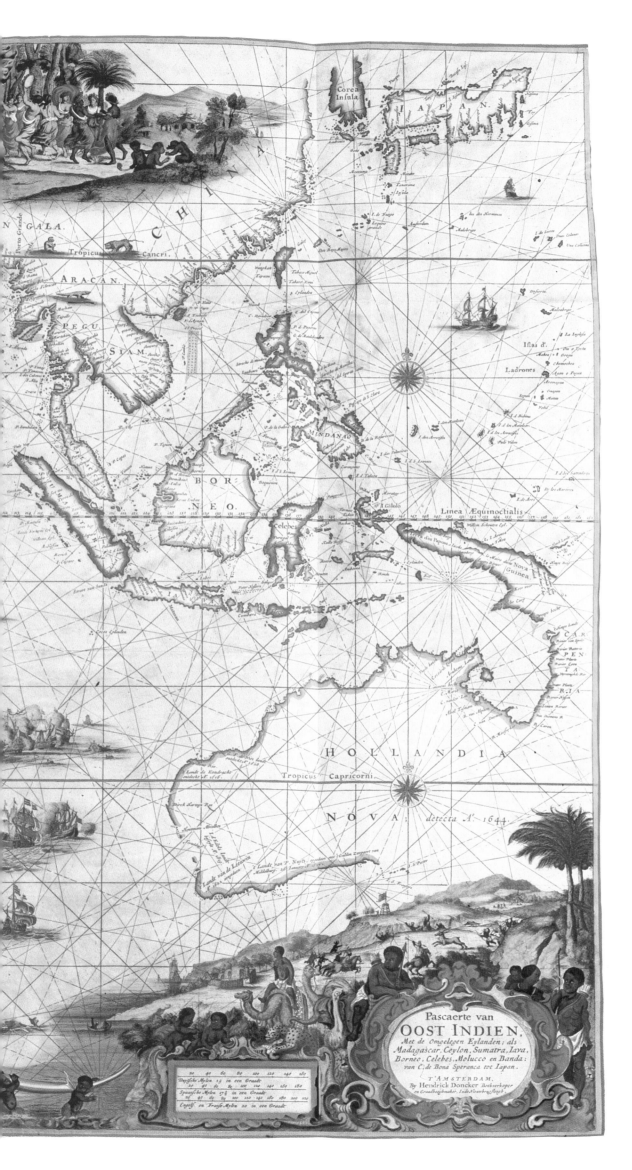

Shortly after their first voyage to the East Indies, the Dutch consolidated all their efforts by forming the Dutch East Indies Company in 1602. The company was granted a monopoly on all trade from and to the East Indies. When Jan Huygens van Linschoten returned to Holland after many years in Portuguese service, he told his compatriots that the position of the Portuguese in the Indian Archipelago was more vulnerable than in other parts of Asia. As a result, the Dutch concentrated on the archipelago and succeeded in ousting the Portuguese from the profitable spice market. In 1601 a Dutch fleet defeated the Portuguese off Bantam on the coast of Java, and from then on the Dutch strengthened their position until they firmly held the spice trade. From Batavia, their stronghold and commercial center, the Dutch started to attack the Portuguese hegemony in other Asian seas. One by one the Portuguese positions were conquered. Ceylon was captured between 1636 and 1645, Malacca followed in 1641. At the end of the seventeenth century only Goa in India and Macao on the Chinese coast remained in Portuguese hands. The Dutch East Indies Company was then at its peak.

As the Dutch had profited by information purloined from the Portuguese, they understood the importance of a policy of secrecy about navigation in Asia. The Dutch East Indies Company had its own hydrographer who kept the "secret atlas" of the company. Their charts and sailing directions were guarded zealously; they were brought aboard when the ships sailed from Holland and were gathered again when they returned. However, there were many complaints of pilots' carelessness. And as with the Portuguese, their secrets did not last.

One of the few charts of the Asian seas printed in seventeenth-century Amsterdam is the small-scale "crossover" of the Indian Ocean, published by Hendrik Doncker. The Portuguese held their strongest positions on the Malabar coast, Ceylon, and Malacca. In two periods, between 1636 and 1645 and between 1654 and 1663, these positions were conquered. Malacca fell after a prolonged blockade in 1641. In 1656 the Portuguese lost their last stronghold on Ceylon, Colombo, and on the Malabar coast. Finally, Cochin was taken in 1663.

This rare sea chart is probably the first edition; we know that Pieter Goos, and later Gerard van Keulen, issued this chart again. It is also one of the earliest charts showing the Dutch discoveries on the west coast of Australia. The exact date of issue is not known, but the chart is mentioned in an advertisement, printed in Doncker's 1664 pilot guide of the Mediterranean.

PLATE 62
Dutch flagship with 96 pieces.
Gerard van Keulen
(Amsterdam, 1734).
Copper engaving on paper.
From the pilot guide
*De Nieuwe Groote Ligtende
Zee-Fakkel, 't Vijfde Deel.*

The first Dutch fleet on its way to the East Indies rounded the Cape of Good Hope and sailed to Mauritius, off Madagascar, to avoid the Portuguese-dominated route along Africa's east coast. After resupplying, they made straight for Java. But on this route they encountered unfavorable southeastern trade winds, and they soon found it preferable to sail on a higher latitude. Between 35 and 40 degrees south, prevailing westerly winds enabled them to make a swift journey to Java. A sailing instruction of 1617 directed pilots to find these Westerlies and to keep an eastern course for at least 1000 miles before turning north to Java. The instructions warned that when the course was altered too early, the ships would come west of Sumatra in the area of unfavorable winds.

Determination of a ship's exact longitude was impossible in those days. That, and the generality of the instructions, produced the error that brought Dutch ships to an important landfall on the west coast of Australia.

The first to do so was the 'Eendracht, under command of Dirck Hartog. After arriving from Amsterdam at Table Bay, he sought the prevailing Westerlies. Sailing too far east, he made a landfall on the Australian continent on October 25, 1616. To commemorate this, Hartog left a pewter plate nailed to a pole before leaving for Java. On February 4, 1697, Willem de Vlaming, commanding three ships in search of an East Indian who had disappeared, made the same landfall and found the plate, which is now preserved in Amsterdam. He left a similar plate, which was found by the Frenchman Hamelin on his expedition in 1801; he did not take it with him. Louis de Freycinet, a member of the 1801 expedition, returned in 1818 on his circumnavigation and brought the plate to Paris, where it remained until 1940. It was presented to the Australian Government and is now preserved in Perth.

The chart of Victor Victorsz, one of Vlaming's companions, depicts the west coast of Australia between 20 degrees 45 minutes and 33 degrees 10 minutes south. It shows the island where Dirck Hartog made his landfall in 1616. A legend on it reads: *Alhier de Schootel gevonden* ("Here the plate was found.") The ships are Vlaming's *Geelvink, de Nijptangk,* and *'t Weseltje.*

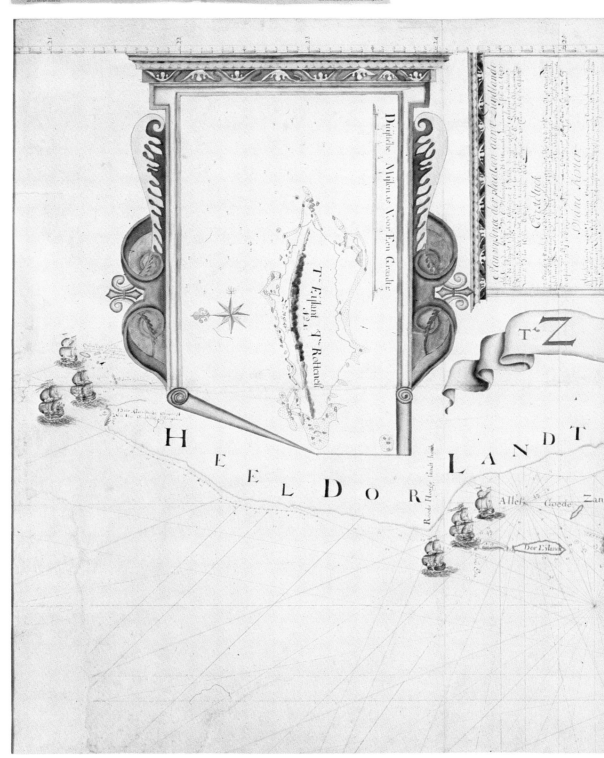

PLATE 63
Chart of the west coast of
Australia.
Victor Victorsz (Batavia,
1697).
28¾ x 59⅞″, manuscript
on paper.

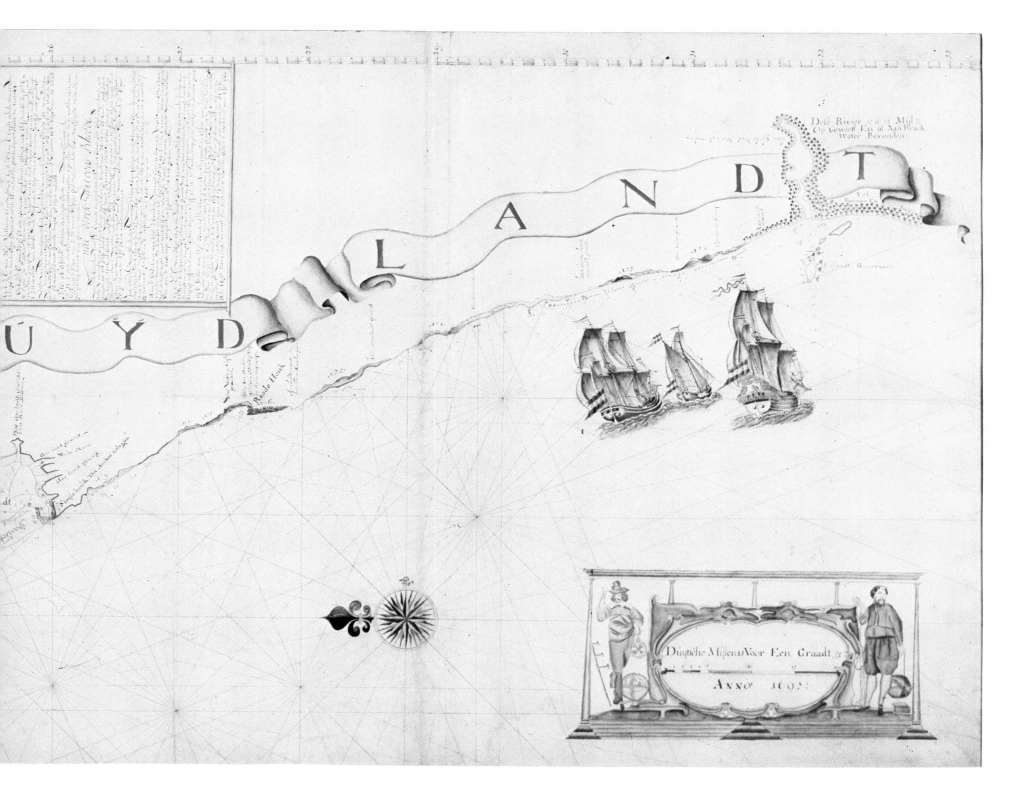

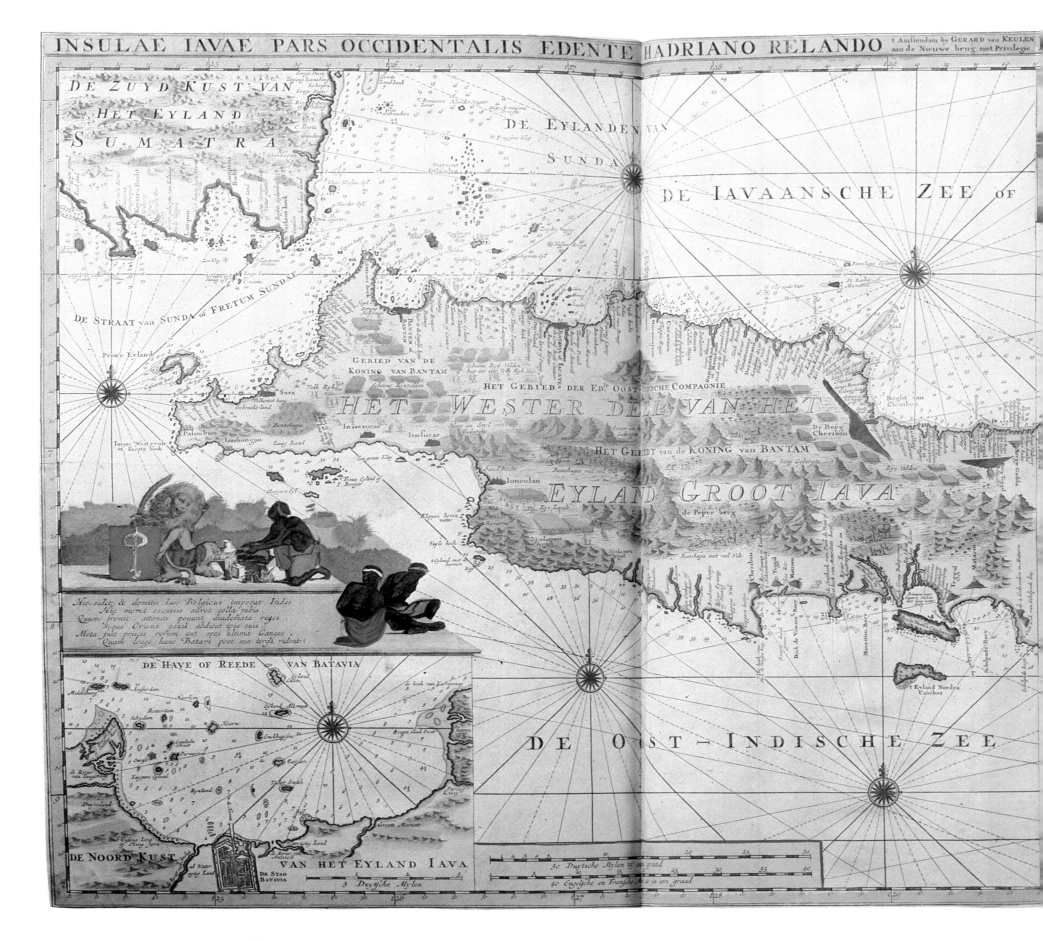

The position of the Portuguese in the islands of the Indian Archipelago was not as strong as it was on the coasts of India and the Moluccas, and the competition of the Dutch was strongly felt soon after their first appearance in the markets of the Spice Islands. In 1601 a Dutch fleet defeated the Portuguese in the vicinity of Bantam, the most important station in the pepper trade on Java.

In 1602 the Dutch consolidated their Asian activities by forming the Dutch East Indies Company, which obtained a monopoly on shipping from Holland to the Indies via the Cape of Good Hope and the Strait of Magellan. The Dutch government granted the company the right to keep its own army and navy, to make alliances, and to administer justice—in short, to behave outside the republic as a sovereign nation. During its existence the Dutch East Indies Company was the biggest and mightiest private enterprise in the world. Highest authority lay with the "Lords XVII" who appointed a governor general to rule the Dutch Indies in their name. The first governor general, Jan Pietersz Coen—his name became the Dutch word for "bold"—founded the fortress Batavia in 1618 near Jakarta on Java's east coast. It became the company's principal city in Asia.

The company's policy was aimed at obtaining a monopolistic position in the spice trade. Nearby Bantam slowly lost its importance after a Dutch blockade and was finally taken in 1684. The im-

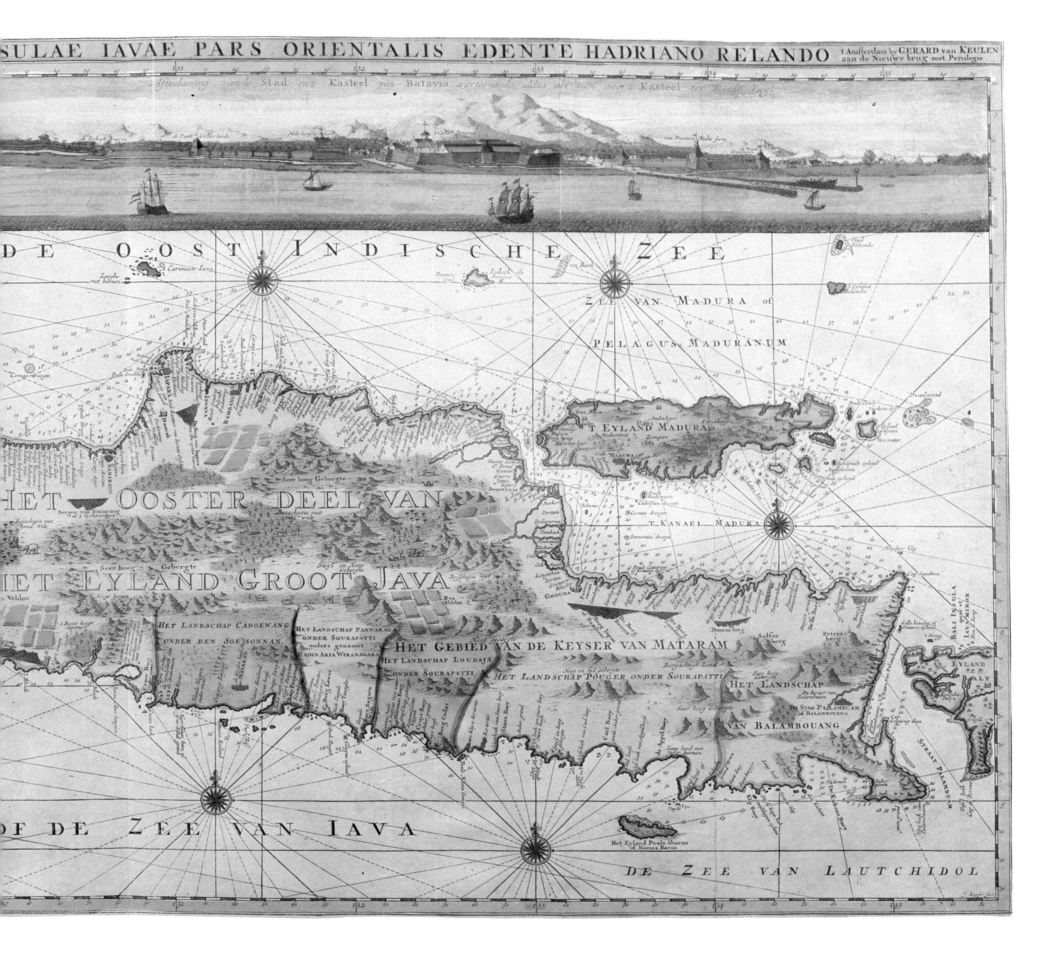

portant kingdom of Mataram also fell, and the English, lacking an organization as strong as the Dutch East Indies Company, were driven from the area around the Spice Islands. In this way the company reached an uncontested position of power in the Indian Archipelago until it was disbanded at the end of the eighteenth century.

Batavia became the most important trading port in the Dutch Indies. There the ships of the yearly Holland-bound fleet were loaded. From Batavia, ships departed to discover and chart the unknown lands, and the material gathered during these voyages was kept at the hydrographical office in Batavia. It was probably there that the manuscript was prepared for the printed chart

of Java published by Gerard van Keulen in 1734.

Negotiations between the Lords XVII of the East Indies Company and the cartographer Johannes Blaeu about publishing a printed sea atlas of the Indian waters in 1667 ended without results, and the embargo on this material was not officially ended until 1753.

The later editions of the fifth part of van Keulen's *Sea Torch* contained a few charts of the Indian seas, anticipating the publication of the sixth and last part, with charts of Asian navigation. One of these was the chart in two parts by Hadrianus Relanus, with a view of the harbor and the city of Batavia.

PLATE 64
Sea chart of the island of Java with the roads and the city of Batavia.
Gerard van Keulen
(Amsterdam, 1734).
20 1/16 x 44 7/8", copper engraving on paper.
From the pilot guide
De Nieuwe Groote Ligtende Zee-Fakkel, 't Vijfde Deel.

119

PACIFIC OCEAN

After crossing the Isthmus of Darien in 1515, Vasco Núñez de Balboa became the first European to see the Pacific. Between 1522 and 1536 the Spanish surveyed the west coast of South America down to Chile. In 1540 Alonso de Camargo sailed through the Strait of Magellan northwards along the west coast.

The name Pizarro is connected forever with the conquest of the Inca Empire. In 1532 Francisco Pizarro landed on the Peruvian coast with 177 soldiers, on foot and mounted, and one small cannon. The vast empire encompassed all the land stretching from Colombia halfway into Chile. Soon armadas with tons of gold and silver sailed from the west coast to Panama, where its cargo was then carried across the isthmus and shipped from Portobello to Spain.

Conquistador Hernando Cortés, after fighting his way through Mexico, founded the Spanish colony of Acapulco on the Pacific Coast. From Acapulco, Cortés sent three ships under the command of his lieutenant, Francisco de Ulloa, in search of these riches. Ulloa charted the Gulf of California, ascertaining that California was a peninsula. But Ulloa was loyal only to his own interests. He sent two of the ships back to Acapulco, and with a small band of adventurers continued his search for the riches of the seven cities of Cibola. He and his party perished wretchedly after their ship was wrecked in a storm.

In 1542–43 Juan Rodriguez Carrillo sailed north along California to Cape Mendocino. On an expedition in the years 1602–3, Sebastian Vizcaino surveyed the coast as far north as forty-three degrees. His companion, Fray Ascension, reported afterwards that they had found California to be an island. Subsequently, for over a century California was wrongly depicted as such.

The beautiful and very decorative chart of America's west coast, from Chile to California, was made by the Portuguese cartographer Diogo Homem and forms part of a portolano atlas commissioned by Queen Mary of England.

Diogo Homem was the son of the cartographer Lopo Homem. As a youth he became involved in a murder case and was banished to Africa. He escaped to England, however, and from there he asked for a pardon. This was granted under the condition that he return to Lisbon, for he was already an accomplished cartographer. There is no evidence that he did so; he is known to have worked instead in Venice and again in London.

Another interesting detail is that one of his clients failed to buy the atlas he had ordered, so Homem went to court. Consequently, we know that two sworn witnesses valued the atlas at 80 and 100 golden ducats, respectively—a small fortune.

PLATE 65
Portolano of the west coast of America.
Diogo Homem (London, 1558).
32⅝ x 23¼", manuscript on vellum.

In a book about seacharts it is appropriate to include the world chart that Gerard Mercator issued in 1569. Although it was an enormous step in the development of the modern sea chart, more than two centuries passed before the Mercator projection chart was generally accepted on board ships. This was largely due to Mercator's failure to explain adequately the manner in which it was constructed and the way it was to be used. In particular, Mercator's contemporaries did not understand how to measure distances on the chart, and we know that Mercator himself was conscious of that deficiency.

At first there were no tables that could be used to calculate the change in latitude near the poles. We do not know exactly how Mercator constructed his chart, but he probably designed it geometrically. Thirty years later the English mathematician Edward Wright devised such tables, and his explanation of the Mercator projection chart stimulated its general use in navigation.

Besides Edward Wright the cartographers Petrus Plancius, Jodocus Hondius, and Willem Jansz Blaeu made the first charts using the Mercator projection. The publication of Blaeu's large world map in 1606 was a milestone in the popularization of Mercator's method.

The part of the world chart depicted here shows the northern area of the Pacific. It is noteworthy because it combines information based upon medieval sources with data Mercator gathered from then contemporary Spanish and Portuguese cartographers. America's coasts, with California depicted as a peninsula, the Philippines, and the Indian Archipelago are more or less correctly shown; it is based upon information gathered by Spanish and Portuguese mariners.

Contrary to these 'modern' parts of the chart, the representation of the coasts of China and Japan contains medieval inaccuracies: the shape of Japan is completely distorted, while Korea is missing altogether.

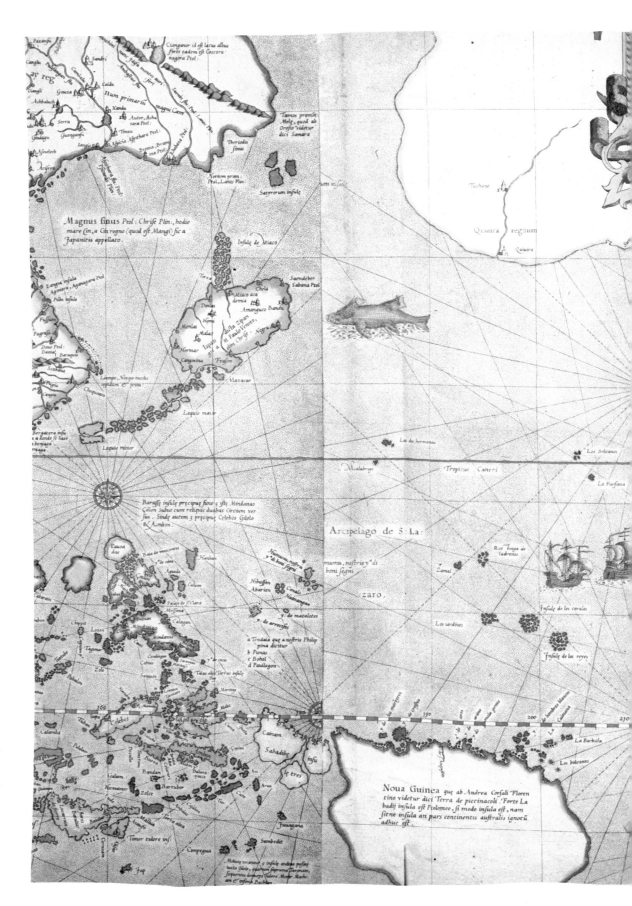

PLATE 66
Sea chart of the northern
Pacific.
Gerard Mercator (Duisburg,
1569).
13³⁄₁₆ x 24³⁄₁₆", copper
engraving on paper.
Part of Gerard Mercator's
world chart.

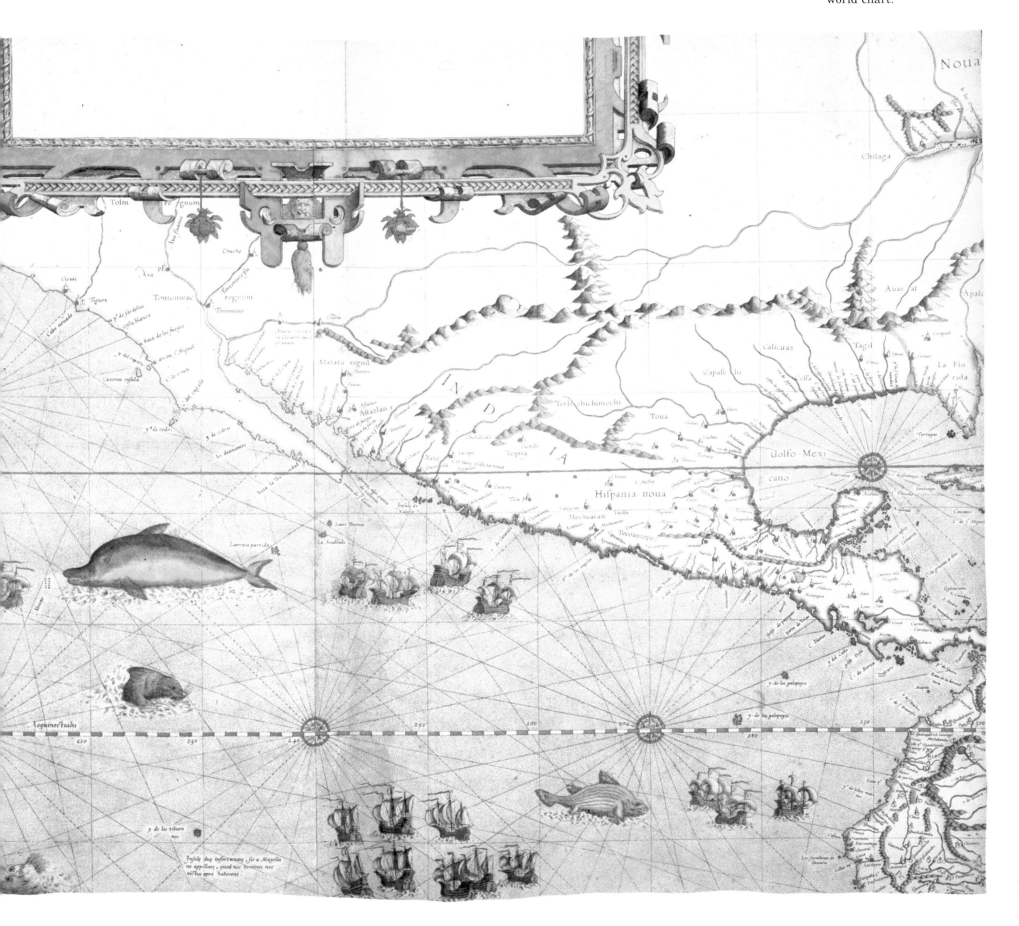

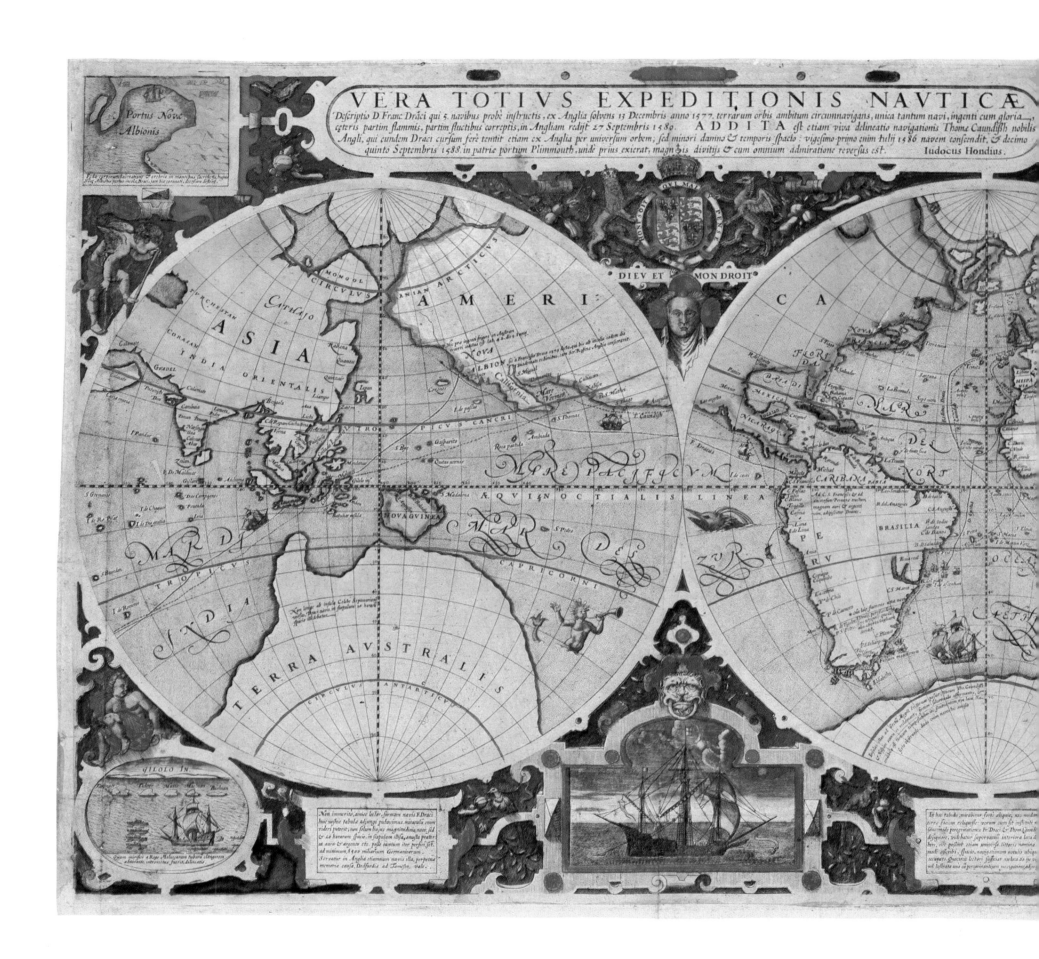

PLATE 67
Chart of the world in two
hemispheres.
Jodocus Hondius (London,
1590).
15¾ x 21⅝", copper
engraving on paper.

The Papal Bull of 1493 divided the land outside Europe between the Spanish and Portuguese thrones. Although all other nations were excluded, the young seafaring countries of Western Europe paid little attention to the papal line of demarcation. Allured by prospects of immense treasures, they continued to search for a route to the magical Spice Islands other than the passage through the Portuguese-dominated Cape of Good Hope.

On one such expedition, the Englishman Francis Drake became the third man—after the Portuguese Magellan and De Loyasa—to circumnavigate the globe. Drake's fleet of five ships left Plymouth Harbour in England on December 13, 1577. Two years and eight months later, laden with gold and spices, they returned to their home port.

The world map in two globes, *Vera Totius Expeditionis Nauticae* by Jodocus Hondius, illustrates the track and events of this remarkable voyage. Drake's ship, the *Golden Hind*, is depicted in the lower middle. Scenes in the four corners relate to the circumnavigation. Drake entered the Pacific via the Strait of Magellan, which separates the South American continent from Tierra del Fuego. After clearing the strait, his ships were driven southward by a fierce storm.

Francis Fletcher, who accompanied the expedition, reported later that open sea existed between America and the magic Southland. Drake was the first European to set eyes on the southernmost point of the American continent, locating it almost correctly at 58 degrees southern latitude. That was twenty-eight years before Schouter and Lemaire sailed into the Pacific south of Tierra del Fuego, naming the Strait of Lemaire and Cape Horn. But the accepted theory that Tierra del Fuego was part of the Southland was so popular that Fletcher's report was ignored. Only Hondius's chart showed this discovery and depicted Tierra del Fuego as a group of islands. Even then, the legend engraved in the Southland indicates the publisher's doubts: "These islands have been placed at the Magellan Strait by Francis Drake. But he is contradicted by Thomas Cavendish and all the Spaniards. It is probable that Drake, driven off course by adverse winds, did not investigate these regions too closely. He even lost two ships here."

Continuing northward along America's west coast, sacking Spanish settlements along the way, Drake searched for the western entrance to the Northwest Passage. Although he reached 48 degrees north, he was forced back by fierce cold. He then remained for some time in a bay on the west coast of North America to recover and refit his ships (inset, upper left). The exact location of this bay, which he named New Albion, is unknown, but it was probably the Bay of San Francisco or Drake's Bay, farther north. When Drake departed, he left a brass plate to commemorate his stay. In 1936, such a brass plate turned up in the vicinity of San Francisco Bay; it caused much excitement among historians, but its authenticity is doubted. The Englishman continued his voyage across the Pacific and reached the Spice Islands in November 1579 (lower left inset: the "Golden Hind" towed into the harbor of Ternate). He returned to England by way of the Cape of Good Hope in September 1580 and was knighted by Queen Elizabeth I for his accomplishments. In addition to having been a commercial success, the voyage uncovered the basic weakness of the vast colonial empires of Spain and Portugal.

PLATE 68
Sea chart of the Pacific.
Hessel Gerritsz
(Amsterdam, 1622).
43⁵/₁₆ x 57⁷/₈″, manuscript
on vellum.

On his fourth and last voyage Columbus sailed along the Caribbean coast of Darien. There he heard stories about a sea on the other side of the isthmus. However, Vasco Núñez de Balboa was the first European to see the Pacific. After crossing the Isthmus of Panama, he reached the top of the Sierra Quaregua on September 25, 1515, and saw the *Mare del Zur*.

Ferdinand Magellan, Portuguese by birth, entered the service of the king of Spain. Having convinced the Spanish that the Moluccas, with their riches, lay in the Spanish sphere of interest, he was outfitted for a voyage of discovery to the west beyond Columbus's New World. On September 20, 1519, he sailed with a fleet of five ships from the harbor of San Lucar to find the western route to the East Indies. After discovering the strait, which now bears his name, at the tip of South America, he entered the *Mare del Pacifico* on December 27, 1520.

Magellan sailed into the Pacific convinced that he had almost reached his goal: a voyage of two, at the most three, weeks would bring him to the Moluccas. But for ninety-nine days he sailed west, driven by an eastern wind, without seeing anything but the vast water. At last, on March 6, 1521, he reached the Ladrones (now called the Marianas). Ten days later he reached the Philippines, where he was killed in a skirmish. After a voyage of three years, only one of the five ships, the *Victoria*, returned, thus completing the first circumnavigation.

Magellan's voyage finally dispelled the belief that the East Indies could be reached by sailing west for a few weeks.

The Dutch East Indies Company had obtained a monopoly on all merchant shipping to the East Indies via the Cape of Good Hope and the Strait of Magellan. For that reason, in 1616 ships under the command of Jacob Lemaire and Willem Schouten searched for and found a passage to the Pacific between Tierra del Fuego and Staten Island, at the southern tip of the American continent. They named this passage Strait Lemaire after the initiator of the expedition, and when they sailed past the southernmost point of the continent, they called it Cape Horn, after their port of departure.

The ships depicted in the lower part of the chart of the Pacific by Hessel Gerritsz are those of Lemaire and Schouten; they replaced the Southland that appeared on earlier charts. The portraits of Balboa, Magellan, and Lemaire are drawn on the American continent.

Hessel Gerritsz succeeded Petrus Plancius as the hydrographer of the Dutch East Indies Company. He held this important office until his death in 1634. He was followed by Willem Jansz Blaeu. The chart belonged to the so-called "secret atlas" of the company. Lower California is correctly depicted here as a peninsula.

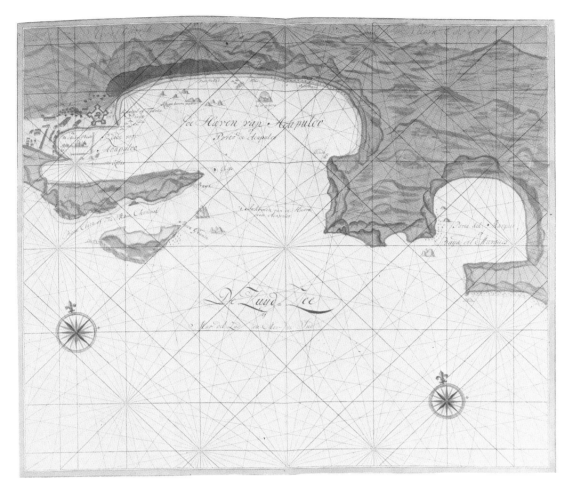

When the Spanish ceased to claim rights over the Moluccas in 1527, they also stopped crossing the Pacific. But in 1564 a Spanish fleet from Chile arrived in Manila Bay and founded the first Spanish colony in the Philippines. When Andres de Urdaneta discovered in northern latitudes a return route to the Americas that enjoyed the Japanese current and the eastern trade winds, regular travel between the Americas and the Far East became possible. Manila developed rapidly into the principal Spanish port for trade with the countries of Southeast Asia. On the American coast, Acapulco was chosen for its favorable location halfway between the zone of the western trade winds and the equatorial currents (16 degrees north latitude).

The Manila-bound galleons would leave Acapulco in March carrying the so-called "silk-money," silver from the Mexican mines to be bartered for Asian products. They would return to Acapulco early the following year with cargos of the Orient's most valuable products: silk, porcelain, lacquerware, ivory, jade, spices, and tea.

Along with the *capitanos* and the *almirantes* of the armadas, the Manila galleons carried the richest cargoes. When Commander Anson captured a galleon bound from Acapulco in 1743, he found it to be carrying, among other treasures, over one and a half million silver pesos.

Johannes Vingboons's collection of sea charts for the voyages to the important islands, towns, and fortresses in the Spanish, English, and Dutch Indies are all drawn from life.

PLATE 69
Chart of the harbor of Acapulco.
Johannes van Keulen II (Amsterdam, 1738).
20¹/₁₆ x 23″, manuscript on paper.
From the pilot guide *De Nieuwe Groote Ligtende Zee-Fakkel, 't Vijfde Deel.*

PLATE 70
View of the port of Acapulco.
Johannes Vingboons (Amsterdam, c. 1650–70).
16⁹/₁₆ x 21⅝″, watercolor on paper.
From the *Vingboons Atlas*, a collection of sea charts and views of harbors outside Europe.

Int Rijck van nova Espanien
ee.

PLATE 71
Portolano of Southeast Asia.
Antonio Sanches (Lisbon,
1642).
17¹⁵⁄₁₆ x 26″, manuscript
on vellum.
From the atlas
*Idrographisiae Nova
Descriptio.*

The Treaty of Tordesillas in 1493 divided the world into Portuguese and Spanish spheres of influence by a line of demarcation 370 leagues west of the Cape Verde Islands. It settled the argument about Spanish or Portuguese dominion in the New World, but the Portuguese pressing east in the Indian Ocean and the Spanish sailing west were bound to meet at the other end of the world. And the most important question was who would get the Moluccas and the spice monopoly.

Magellan, then serving Spain, believed that the Moluccas lay in the Spanish sphere. He apparently accepted Francisco Serrao's boasts about the distance he had sailed east on his voyage of discovery from Malacca to the Moluccas.

It seems that the Portuguese cartographer Jorge Reinel, at that moment exiled in Seville, had prepared a chart with the Moluccas in the Spanish sphere, contrary to fact and to the interests of his own country. He was brought back by his father, Pedro Reinel, and supported the Portuguese case from then on.

Trying to prove that the Moluccas were theirs, both nations used the service of their most outstanding cartographers. The Spaniards tried without success to bring both Reinels into the service of the Spanish king. The affair was settled in 1529 at the Junta of Rajadoz-Elvas, when Spain ceded its claims to the Portuguese for a sum of 350,000 gold ducats. Afterward the Pacific between the Americas and the Philippines became a Spanish sea, while the Portuguese maintained their hegemony in Asia.

The manuscript chart of the Far East depicted here is by the Portuguese cartographer Antonio Sanches. We know only that he worked between 1623 and 1641. The chart forms part of an atlas that also contains a number of charts by Giovanni Baptista Cavalini.

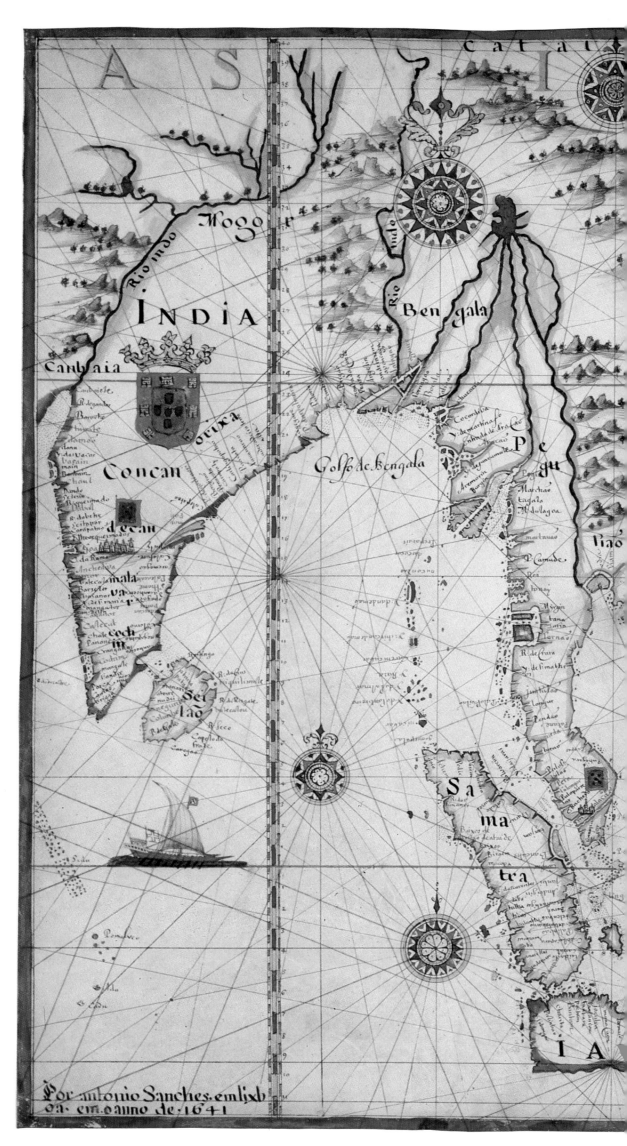

With the exception of charts by explorers, all charts are to some extent copies of other charts with additions and amendments by the makers. For this reason a discoverer's mistake sometimes lives a long life. A well-known example is the mapping of California. In the first maps it is correctly shown as a peninsula, but after an incorrect report, it was wrongly depicted for over a century as an island. The opposite happened in the charting of the northernmost island of Japan—Hokkaido or Yezo—and Kuriles, and the island of Sakharin, directly north of it.

The manuscript chart from the archives of the Dutch East Indies Company, now preserved at the State Archives at The Hague, resulted from a voyage the *Castricum* made in 1643 under the command of Maarten Gerritsz Vries. In those days western knowledge of Japan was restricted to its southern part. In 1609 the Dutch had established a factory at Hirado on Kyushu, the southernmost island of Japan, and beginning in 1641 the bridge between their factory on the little island of Decima and the city of Nagasaki was the only link between Europe and Japan. Only a vague notion of the lands northeast of Japan's main island existed. Nevertheless, Yezo was correctly depicted as an island in the influential map of the Jesuit Matteo Ricci, which Vries took with him when he departed Batavia in search of the Strait of Anian—the supposed passage from the Arctic into the Pacific Ocean. He sailed on a northeastern course along the east coast of Yezo, passed between the two southernmost islands of the Kuriles, which he named State Land and Companies Land, and surveyed the coast on a northwestern course. Unfortunately he missed the strait between the two islands of Yezo and Sakharin and returned to the Kuriles believing that he had charted the coast of a peninsula of the Asian continent.

Vries made a second error by suggesting the existence of a mainland that he called "Companies Land." These misconceptions are shown on all charts of the Pacific until the explorations of La Parouse in 1787.

PLATE 72
Sea chart of the northern island of Japan and the area directly north of it.
Maarten Gerritsz Vries (Batavia, 1643).
20½ x 28¾", manuscript on paper.

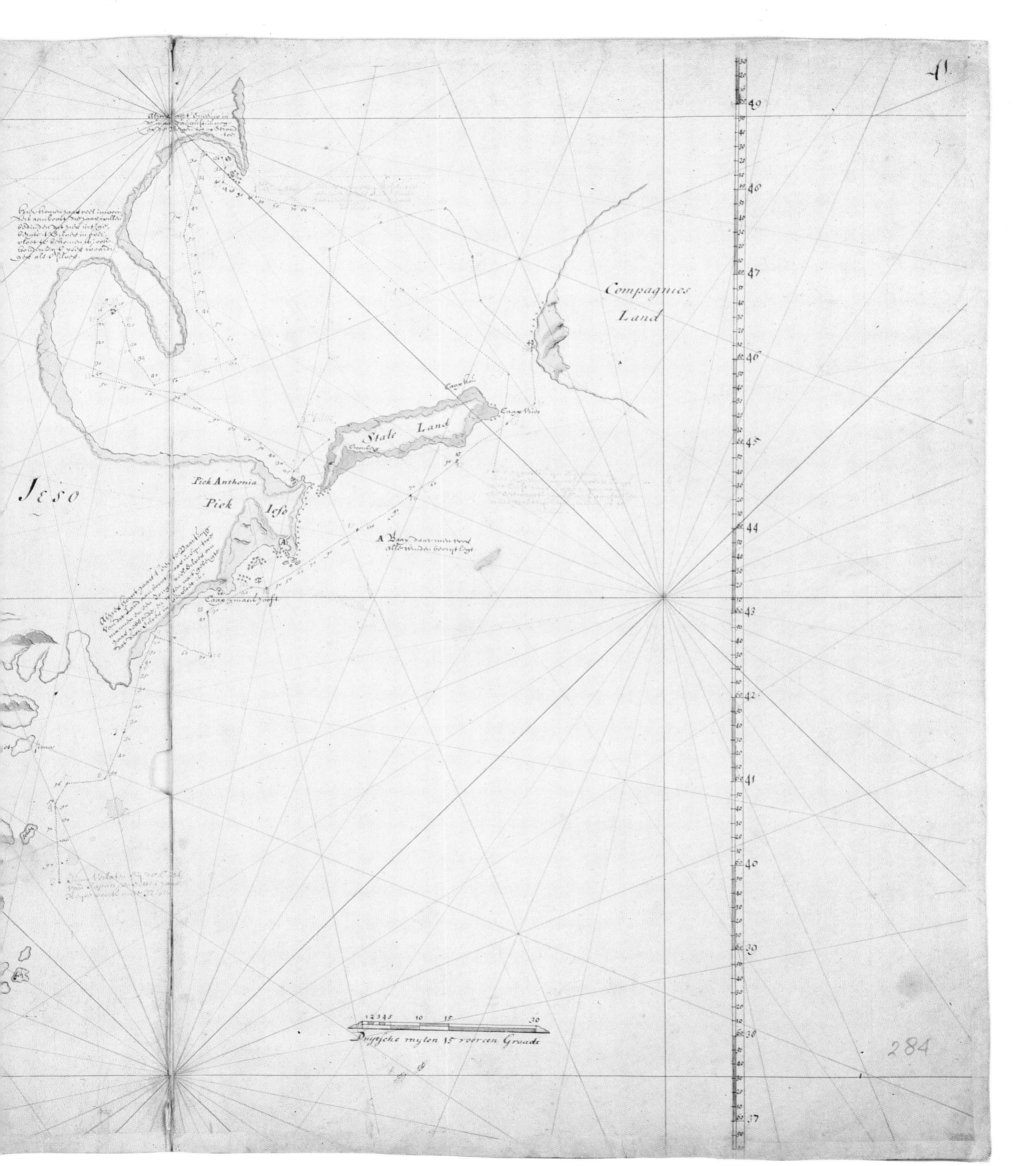

Compagnies
Land

Stale   Land

Pick Anthonia

JESO

Pick   Iefo

Caap maackhooft

A Baar daar onder voet
alle winden beweegt light

Duytfche mylen 15 voor een Graade

49

48

47

46

45

44

43

42

41

40

39

38

37

284

133

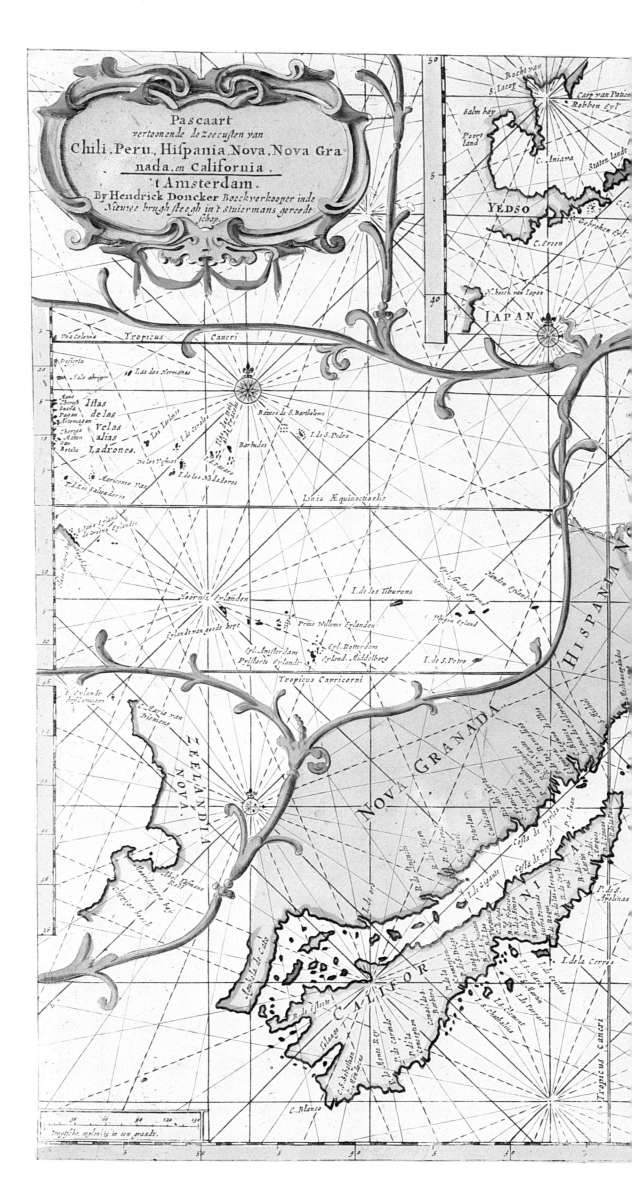

When we look at a chart nowadays, we expect to find North at the top. When this is not the case, we are easily confused and may not recognize a part of the world otherwise familiar to us. In earlier times there was no such convention; the given measurements of the chart in an atlas determined how the area was depicted.

Land area is of little importance in a sea chart and is therefore left blank. Sometimes this space is used for giving additional information and is covered with insets showing adjoining coastal waters. This is certainly the case with the interesting chart of the west coast of America by the Dutch cartographer Hendrik Doncker. The main chart covers the coast from Chile to California, while the insets show the coasts of Asian Russia and Japan, part of the East Indies, and "Nova Zeelandia." To our way of thinking, this chart is upside down: North is indicated by the fleur-de-lys of the compass. East was often indicated by a cross, referring to the Holy City.

Hendrik Doncker (1636–1699) had a shop near the waterfront of Amsterdam named *'in 't Stuurmans Gereetschap* ("In the Mariners Instruments"). He was one of the most prolific publishers of nautical works in seventeenth-century Amsterdam. From 1655 on he and Pieter Goos, Casparus, and Jacob Antoniesz Lootsman published a pilot guide named the *Zeespiegel*. After 1664 he published his own pilot guide, the *Neuw Groot Stuurmans Zeespiegel*. Unlike his pilot guide, his sea atlas, *Zee-atlas ofte Water-Waereld*, first published in 1651, stood on its own. The number of charts increased from nineteen in the first edition to fifty. Unlike the charts of most of his competitors, Doncker's were original and were updated regularly; obsolete charts were replaced by new ones.

In 1660, pressed by the success of Pieter Goos's *Zee-Atlas*, he issued the *Nieuwe Groote Vermeerderde Zee-atlas* with fifty enlarged sea charts. This beautiful atlas was improved over the next twenty-five years. Upon his death in 1699 his stock was sold to Johannes van Keulen.

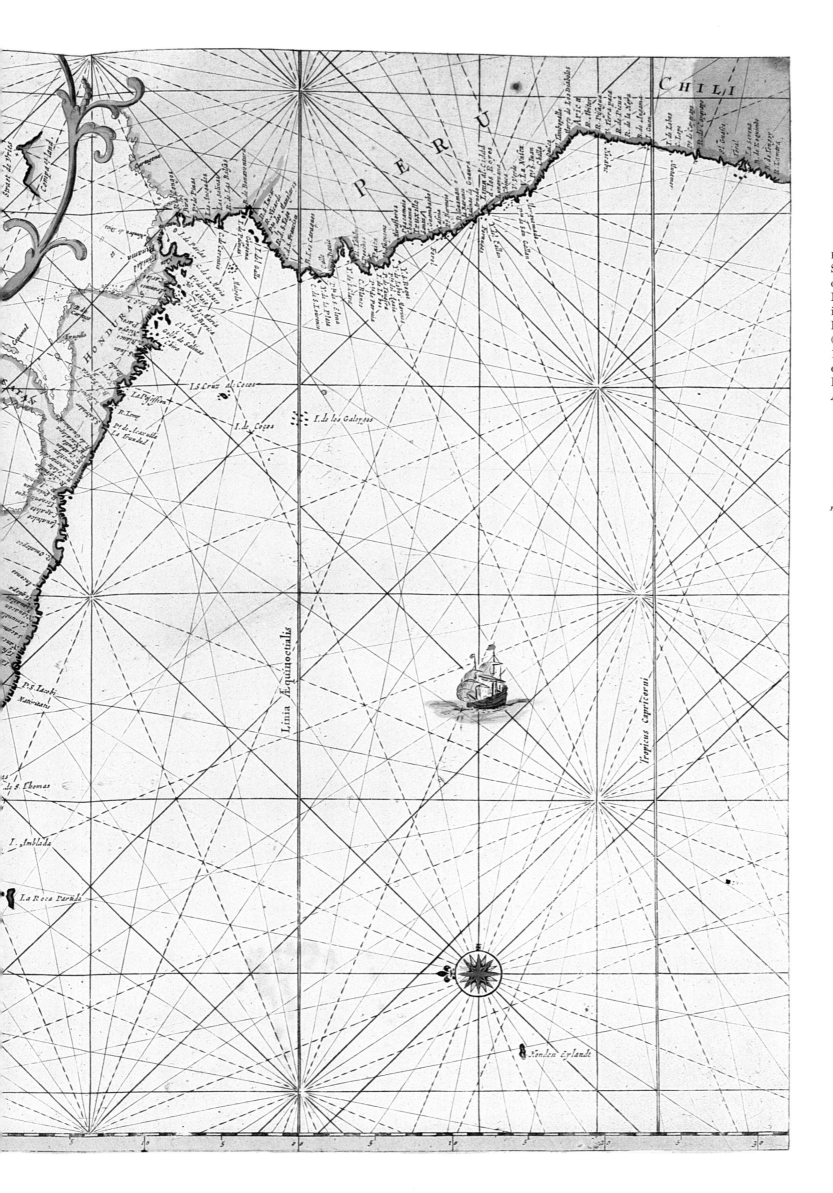

PLATE 73
Sea chart of the west coast
of America with Japan, the
Marianas, and New Zealand
in the insets.
Hendrik Doncker
(Amsterdam, 1660).
16¹⁵/₁₆ x 21¼", copper
engraving on paper.
From the atlas *The Sea
Atlas of the Water World.*

135

ATLAS FRONTISPIECES

Many of the charts reproduced in this book have been taken from sea atlases, enormous volumes containing anywhere from ten to more than one hundred different charts. Most of the atlases that have survived the ages are now in the collections of museums and libraries, since many of those once owned by private collectors have been cut up and the charts sold separately.

The atlases contain beautiful frontispieces with generally allegorical illustrations depicting mythological figures like Neptune, the god of the sea, and Mercury, the god of commerce. They also frequently portray mermaids, sea monsters, ships, and navigational instruments, as well as the products and inhabitants of foreign countries. Three frontispieces are reproduced on the following pages: the first is from the celestial atlas *Atlas Coelestis* by Andreas Cellarius; the second is that of a sea atlas published by Romeijn de Hooghe; and the last is taken from the sea atlas by Johannes Loots.

These sea atlases also contained title pages giving information about the atlas itself. Unfortunately, the information is generally incomplete and seldom gives exact details about who designed the charts, who cut the copperplates, and who made the illustrations. Archival research is now generally the only way to obtain such information. The history of the production of charts, atlases, and pilot guides in the 17th-century Amsterdam gives an idea of how complicated this research can be. Publishers were fierce rivals, and yet on occasion they also cooperated. Copyrights were protected by decisions of the government, either of the "Staaten Generaal" of the Dutch republic or of the provincial "Staaten." The words *Cum priviligio* together with the number of years for which the copyright was valid (generally fifteen) were printed in the atlas or pilot guide as well as on each chart. After the copyright expired, other publishers were allowed to publish the book or the chart. This happened, for instance, to Willem Blaeu after the publication of his very successful pilot guide *Licht der Zeevaerdt*. When the copyright expired in 1618, Johannes Janssonius published his edition of the guide in 1620. Janssonius's edition was an exact copy of Blaeu's guide.

Publishers also frequently purchased the copperplates for atlases published by their rivals. The plates for the charts in Frederick de Wit's *Atlas Maritime*, for instance, were owned after his death by Louis Renard, Reinier and Joshua Ottens, and the widow of Gerard Hulst van Keulen. The last documented use of the plates was for an atlas published a full century after the first edition of the *Atlas Maritime*.

The *Zeespiegel* provides another example of how complex the histories of sea atlases and pilot guides can be. Antonie Jacobsz was the first to publish a pilot guide by this title. After his death, Pieter Goos brought the copperplates and used them for his *Zeespiegel*. At the same time, Johannes Janssonius sold Goos's pilot guide under his own imprint. Meanwhile, the sons of Antonie Jacobsz, Jacob Antoniesz and Casparus Lootsman, copied their father's copperplates and also published a pilot guide with the title *Zeespiegel*. But we have not finished yet, for to complicate things even further, Hendrik Doncker copied Pieter Goos's copperplates and put out still another edition of the *Zeespiegel*.

It also happened that different publishing houses published each other's work. Jacobus Robijn, for example, published the English edition of Lootsman's *Zeespiegel*. Still another complicating factor in the history of sea charts was the practice of publishers buying individual charts from other publishers and then having them hand-colored and bound. A sea atlas by Pieter Goos, for example, was published as part of Johannes Blaeu's *Atlas Mayor* with added charts by Willem and Johannes Blaeu, and the atlas also mentions the addresses of Jacobus Robijn and Hendrik Doncker.

Publishers' names provide a further source of confusion. To distinguish themselves from others, Antonie Jacobsz and his sons added *Lootsman*—at that time the Dutch word for *pilot*—to their names. Unfortunately, this gave rise to the belief that they were related to the publisher Johannes Lootsman or Lootzman, which in fact they were not. In short, the genealogy of sea charts is extremely complex.

ATLAS COELESTIS;
seu
HARMONIA
MACROCOSMICA.

PLATE 74
Frontispiece of the celestial
atlas *Atlas Coelestes.*
Andreas Cellarius and
Johannes Janssonius
(Amsterdam, 1660).

ATLAS
MARITIME

Non pius Æneas, non sic erraßet Ulyßes
Carpußßet rectum per mare, Typhys iter
Si duxißet Atlas, latraret Scylla Sirenes
Cantarent frustra, cocoasq; ad littora rupes
Per vada per syrtes, cocoasq; ad littora rupes
Edocet Oceano quælibet ire vias.
Deßide Neme, Gallus, Britonna regna,
Quæ Batavum, captat Marte vel arte magis.
Nec atavum reparate decus, nec cedite Gallo
Floreat Herculeus, Dædalusq; labor.

Romanus de Hooghe J.U.D. et
Com. Reg. tab. hane suis
Delebit auct. et inv. 1693

A AMSTERDAM Chez *PIERRE MORTIER.*

PLATE 75
Frontispiece of the sea atlas
Atlas Maritime.
Romeijn de Hooghe/Pieter
Mortier (Amsterdam, 1694).

AMSTELODAMI EX OFFICINA IOHANNES LOOTZ
Cum Privilegio Ordinum Hollandiæ et Westfrisiæ.

PLATE 76
Frontispiece of sea atlas *Het
Nieu en Compleet Paskaart
Boek van de Noord en Oost-
Zee.*
Johannes Loots
(Amsterdam, 1697).

139

LIST OF PLATES

FURTHER READING

BOOKS

Bagrow, Leo. *History of Cartography*. Revised and enlarged by R. A. Skelton. Translated by D. L. Paisey. Cambridge: Harvard University Press, 1964.

Cumming, William P.; Skelton, R. A.; and Quinn, D. B. *The Discovery of North America*. New York: American Heritage Press, 1972.

Howse, Derek, and Sanderson, Michael. *The Sea Chart*. New York: McGraw-Hill, 1973.

Johnson, Adrian Miles. *America Explored: A Cartographical History of the Exploration of North America*. New York: Viking Press, 1974.

Tooley, Ronald Vere. *Maps and Map Makers*. New York: Crown, 1970.

————. *Tooley's Dictionary of Map Makers*. Tring, Hertfordshire, England: Map Collector Publications, 1979.

Scammel, Geoffrey Vaughn. *The World Encompassed: The First European Maritime Empires, 800–1650*. Berkeley: University of California Press, 1981.

Schwartz, Seymour I., and Ehrenberg, Ralph E. *The Mapping of America*. New York: Harry N. Abrams, 1980.

Waters, David Watkin. *The Art of Navigation in England in Elizabethan and Early Stuart Times*. New Haven: Yale University Press, 1958.

————, ed. *The Rutters of the Sea*. Pierre Garcie, called Ferrande, original author. New Haven: Yale University Press, 1967.

Wynter, Harriet, and Turner, Anthony. *Scientific Instruments*. New York: Scribners, 1975.

PERIODICALS

Imago Mundi: The Journal of the International Society for the History of Cartography. London, 31 volumes issued to date.

The Map Collector. Tring, Hertfordshire, England, 12 numbers issued to date. Quarterly journal.

ACKNOWLEDGMENTS

The author wishes to express his thanks to the
museums and libraries that granted permission
to reproduce charts from their collections. Also
to Dr. P. Koster of Amsterdam.
In particular, the author expresses his grati-
tude to Mrs. E. Bos-Rietdijk of the Prince Hendrik Maritime Museum; Mr. P. J. Puypen of the
State Maritime Museum of The Netherlands; Dr.
D. de Vries of the Library of the University of
Leiden; Dr. J. Werner of the Library of the University of Amsterdam; and Dr. K. Zandvliet of
the General State Archives at The Hague, for
their helpful assistance.

The plates that appear in this book come from
the collections of the following maritime museums and libraries:

Bibliotheque National, Paris: plates 1, 2, 10, 48,
56, 57, 68

British Library, London: plates 11, 12, 17, 22, 65

General State Archives, The Hague: plates 4, 13,
15, 16, 23, 28, 49, 63, 70, 72

Collection of Dr. Peter Koster, Amsterdam: plate
27

Library of the Ministry of Defense, Paris: plate 14

Library of the University of Amsterdam, Amsterdam: plates 5, 6, 19, 20, 45, 50

Library of the University of Leiden, Leiden:
plates 8, 25, 26, 39, 55, 75

Museum Meermanno Westreenianum, The
Hague: plates 41, 53, 54, 61

National Maritime Museum, Greenwich: plates
3, 52

Prince Hendrik Maritime Museum, Rotterdam:
plates 7, 9, 18, 29, 30, 31, 32, 33, 34, 35, 36,
37, 38, 40, 41, 42, 43, 44, 47, 51, 59, 60, 62, 64,
66, 67, 69, 73, 74, 76

Private Collection: plate 21

Royal Library, The Hague: plates 46, 58, 71

State Maritime Museum of the Netherlands,
Amsterdam: plate 24